T0111773

CONNECTION

CONNECTION

Meditations & Inspirations

MANDALA

SAN RAFAEL · LOS ANGELES · LONDON

THE PERSON WHO TRIES TO LIVE ALONE WILL NOT SUCCEED AS A HUMAN BEING.

PEARL S. BUCK

IS THERE ANYONE SO WISE AS TO LEARN BY THE EXPERIENCE OF OTHERS?

VOLTAIRE

To get the full value of joy, you must have somebody to divide it with.

MARK TWAIN

We have all known the long loneliness, and we have learned that the only solution is love and that love comes with community.

DOROTHY DAY

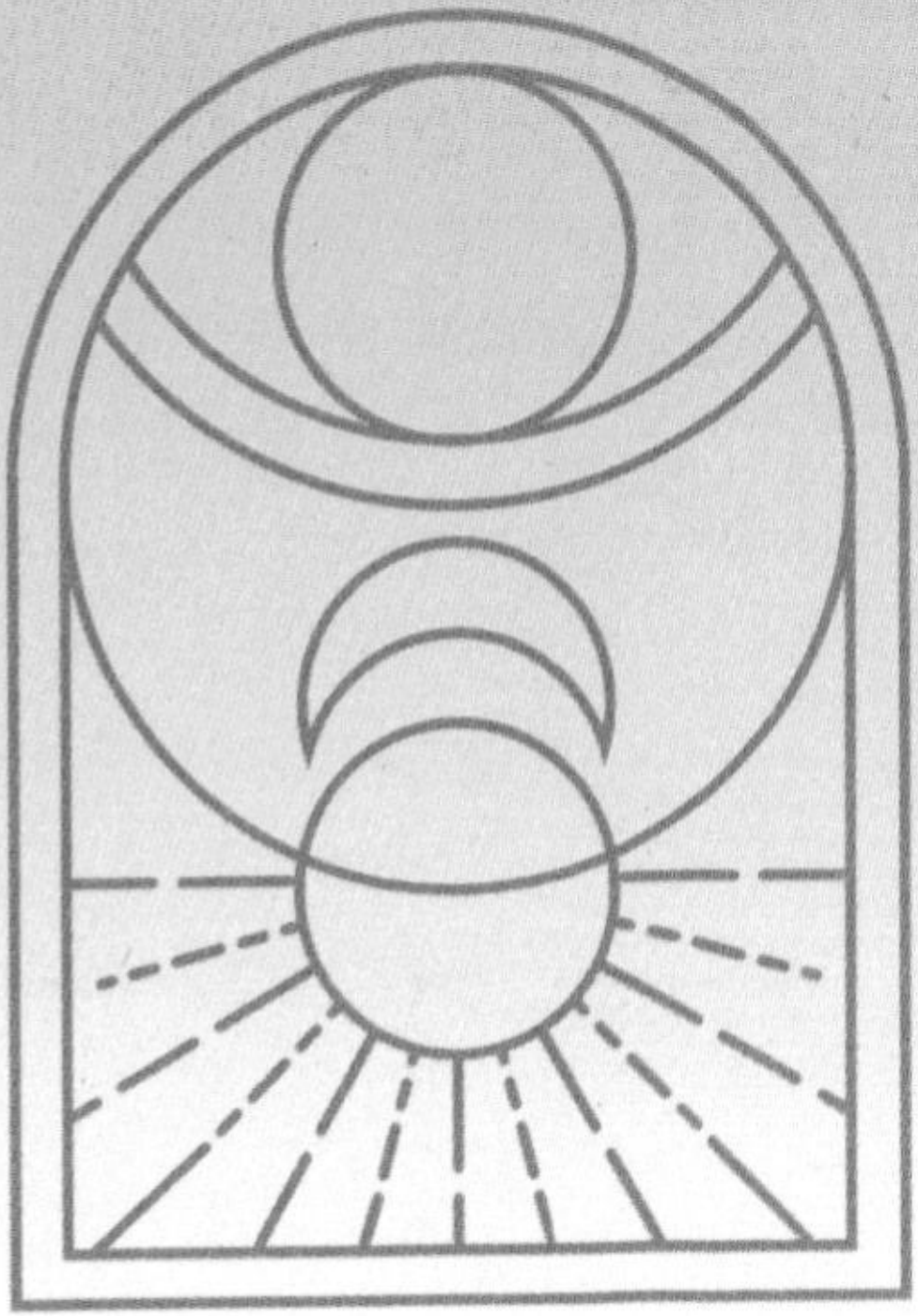

ONE WHO KNOWS HOW TO SHOW AND TO ACCEPT KINDNESS WILL BE A FRIEND BETTER THAN ANY POSSESSION.

SOPHOCLES

FRIENDSHIP is based on the oldest and most intrinsic human awareness that there is more to life than just ourselves.

CHRISTOPHER HANSARD

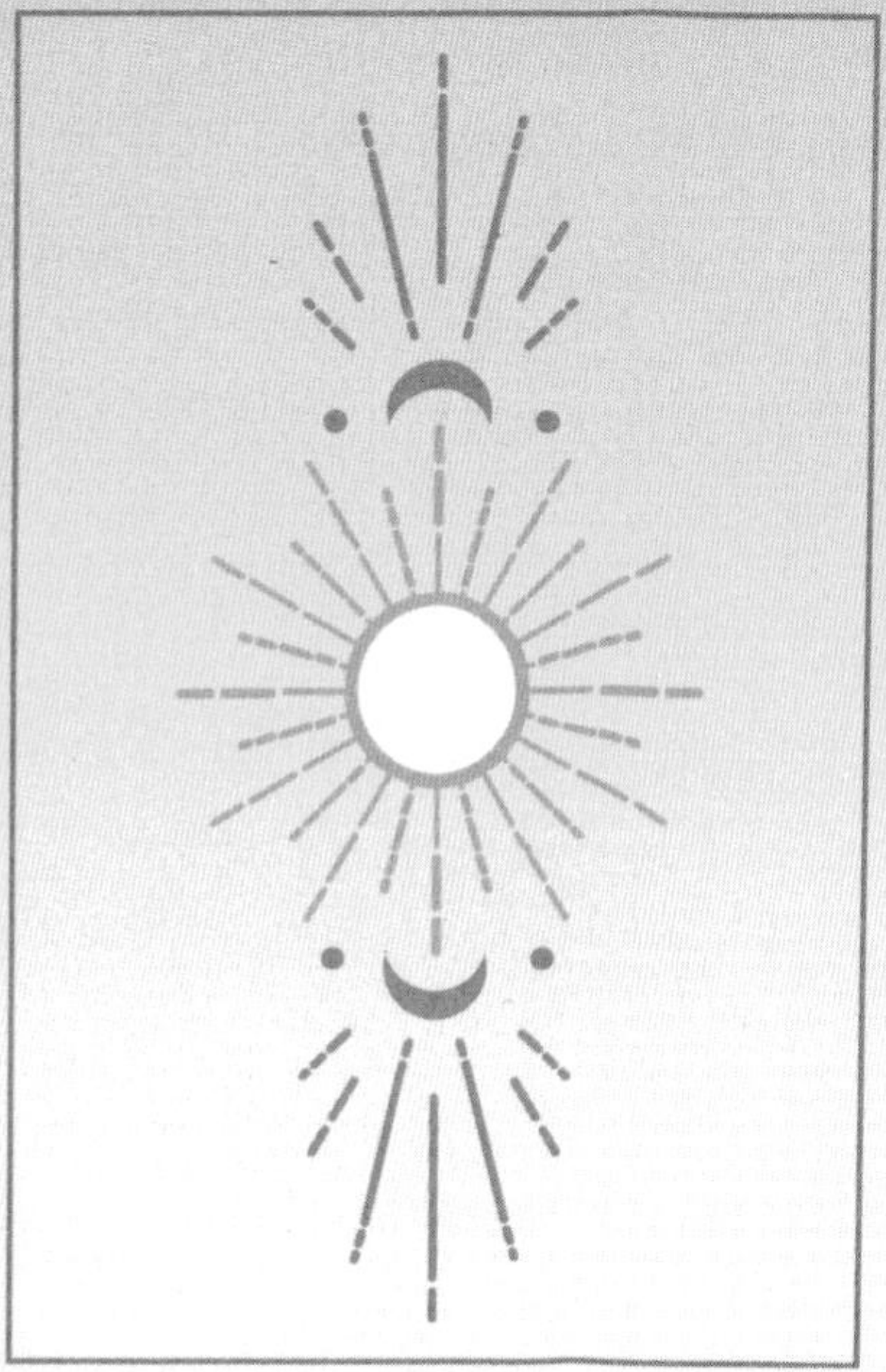

SHARING
what you have is more
IMPORTANT
than what you have.

ALBERT M. WELLS, JR.

When we feel love and kindness towards others, it not only makes others feel loved and cared for, but

it helps us also
to develop
inner happiness
and peace.

DALAI LAMA XIV

I KNOW THERE IS **STRENGTH** IN THE DIFFERENCES BETWEEN US. I KNOW THERE IS **COMFORT** WHERE WE OVERLAP.

ANI DIFRANCO

I have begun to wonder if the secret of living well is not in having all the answers but in pursuing unanswerable questions in good company.

RACHEL NAOMI REMEN

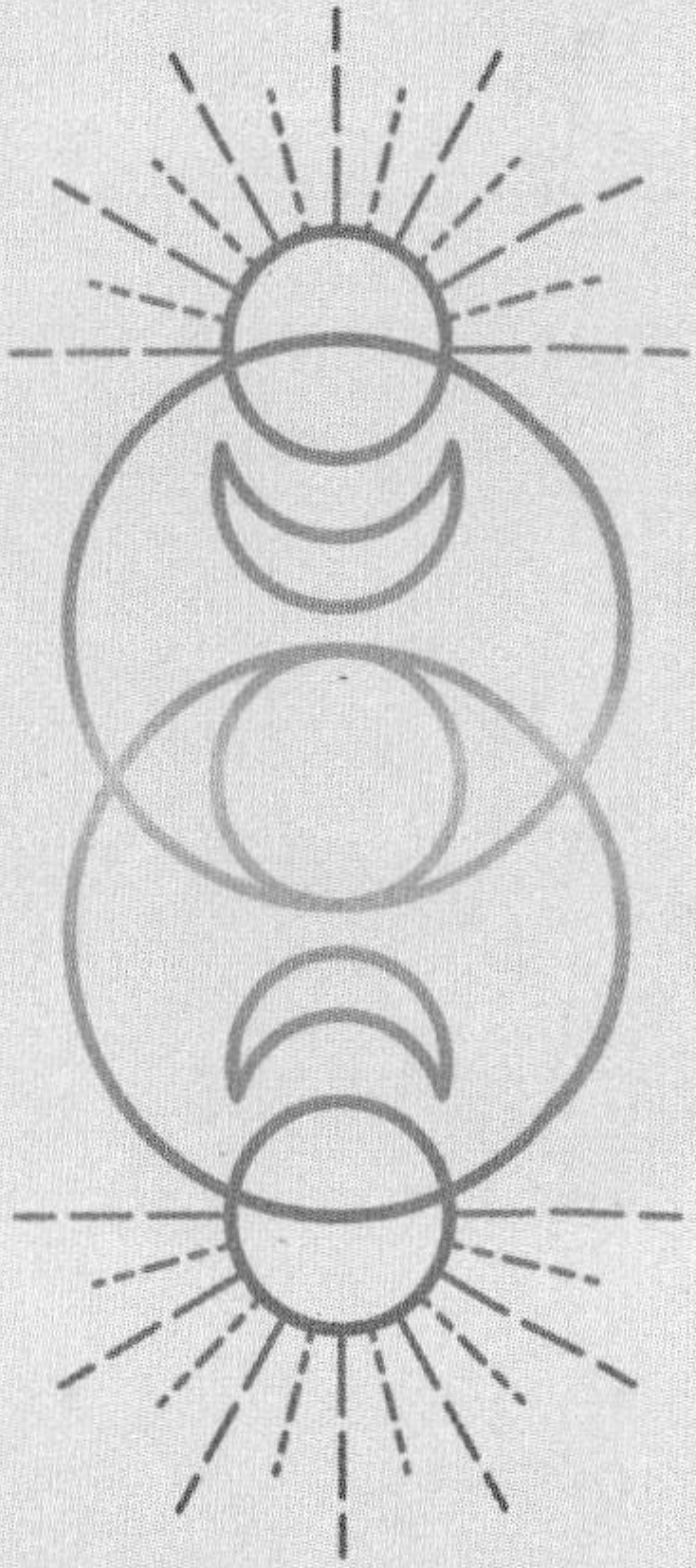

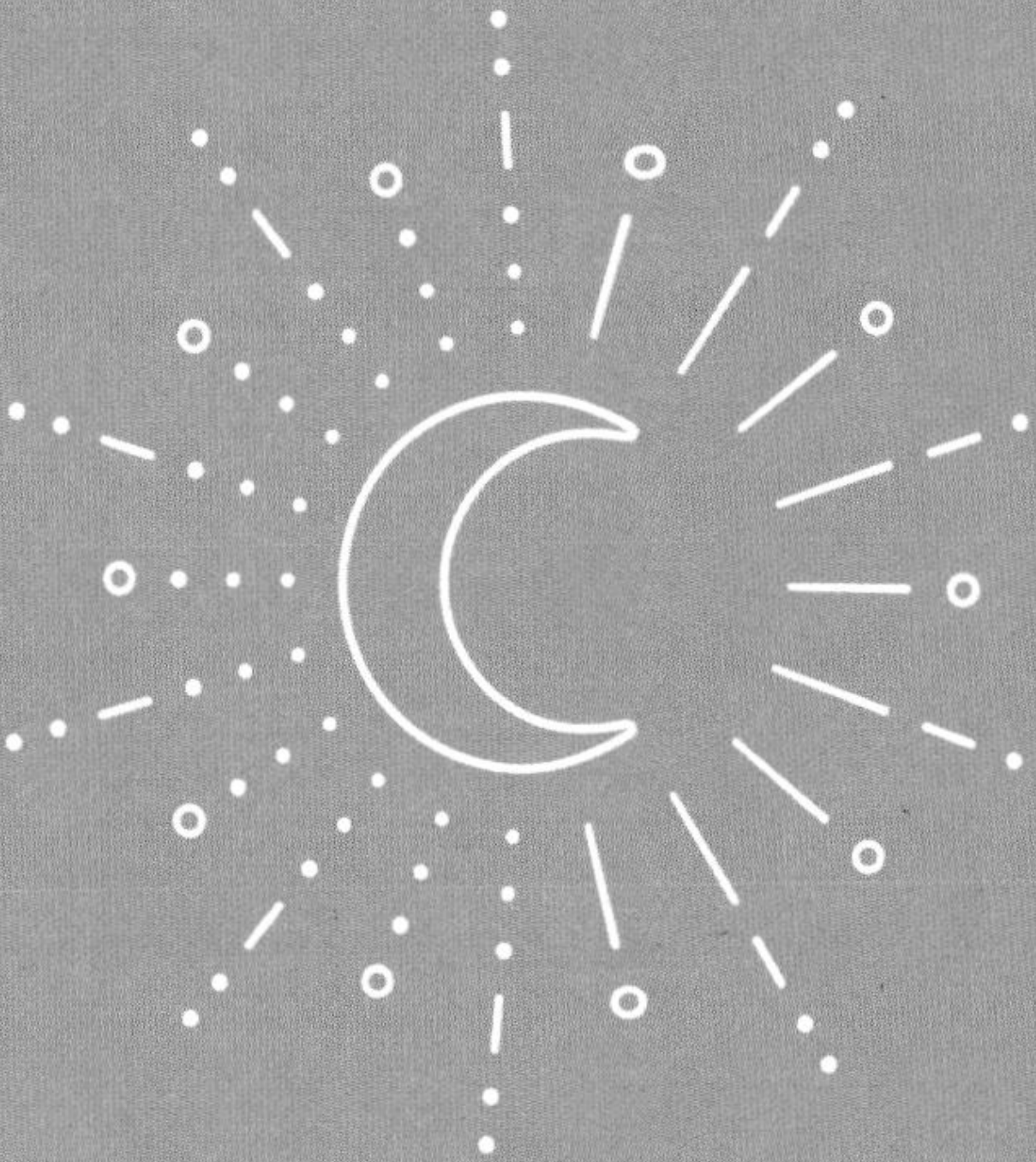

In nature we never see anything isolated, but everything in connection with something else which is before it, beside it, under it, and over it.

JOHANN WOLFGANG VON GOETHE

Whatever affects one directly, affects all indirectly. For some strange reason, I can never be what I ought to be until you are what you ought to be.

MARTIN LUTHER KING, JR.

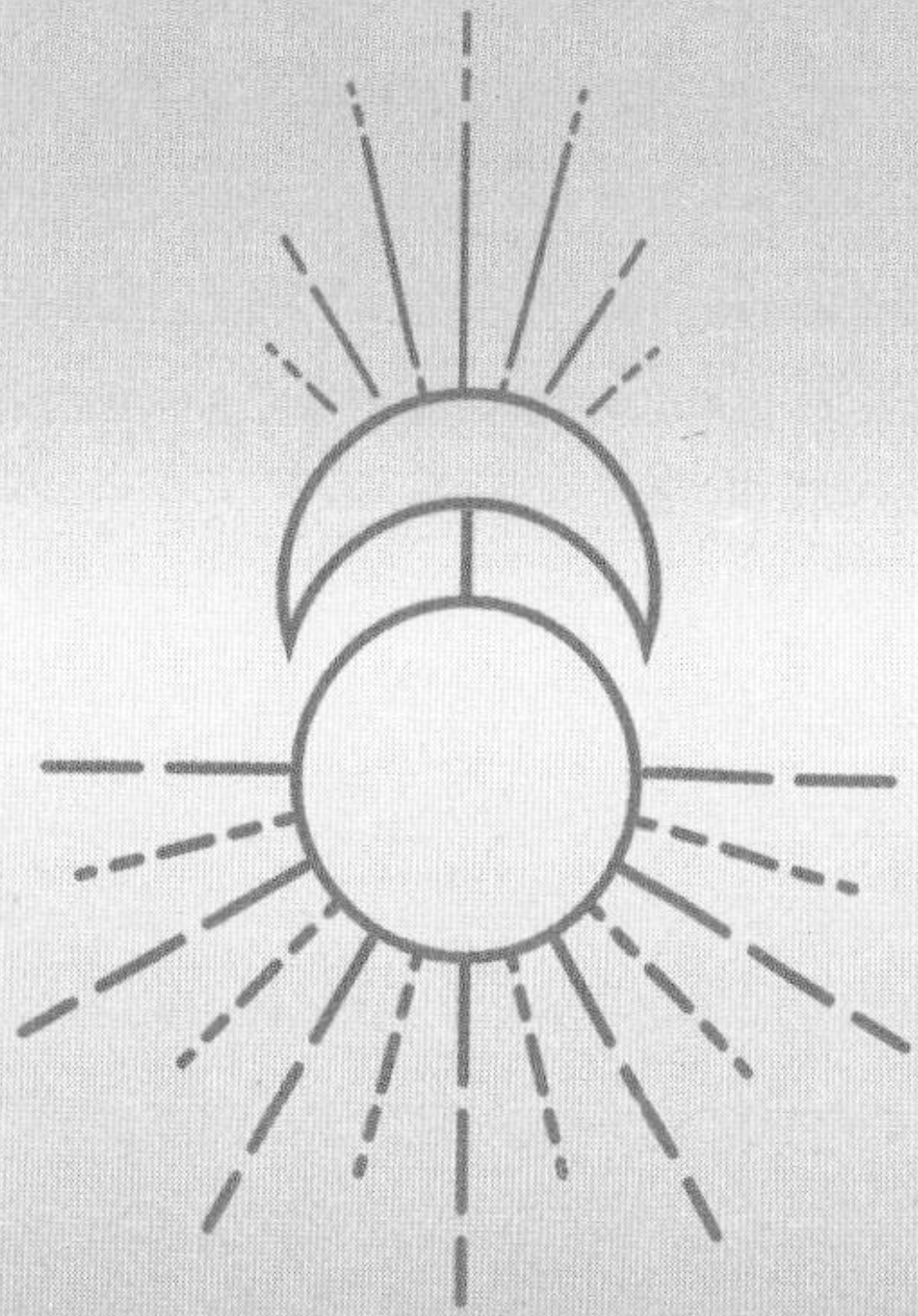

If we have no peace, it is because we have forgotten that we belong to each other.

MOTHER TERESA

For a community to be whole and healthy, it must be based on people's love and concern for each other.

MILLARD FULLER

Your destiny is bound with the destiny of others.

ANDREW BOYD

Remember, we all stumble, everyone of us. That's why it's a comfort to go hand in hand.

EMILY KIMBROUGH

We do not find the meaning of life by ourselves alone—we find it with another.

THOMAS MERTON

We are never
so defenseless
against suffering
as when we love.

SIGMUND FREUD

EVERYONE
NEEDS
HELP FROM
EVERYONE.

BERTOLT BRECHT

ATTENTION IS VITALITY. IT CONNECTS YOU WITH OTHERS. IT MAKES YOU EAGER. STAY EAGER.

SUSAN SONTAG

There is immense power when a group of people with similar interests gets together to work toward the same goals.

IDOWU KOYENIKAN

IT IS IMPOSSIBLE TO TRY ONE'S FRIENDS OUT IN ADVANCE.

MARCUS TULLIUS CICERO

The reason it hurts so much to separate is because our souls are connected.

NICHOLAS SPARKS

When watching after yourself, you watch after others. When watching after others, you watch after yourself.

BUDDHA

True friendship is self-love at second hand.

WILLIAM HAZLITT

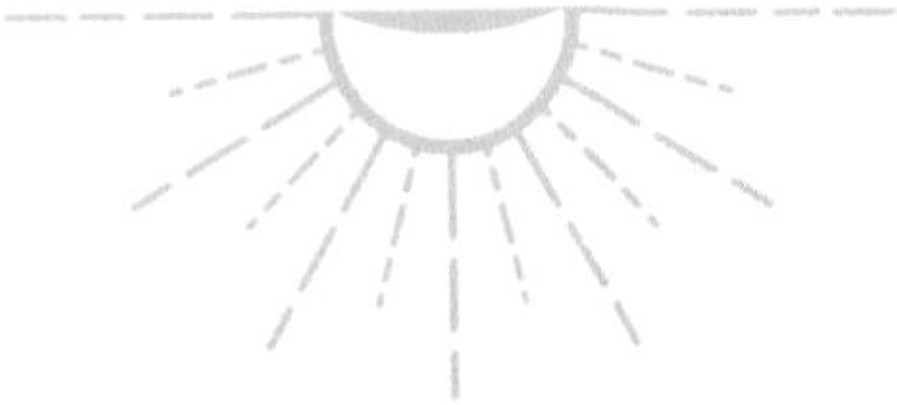

What is a friend? A single soul dwelling in two bodies.

ARISTOTLE

I define connection as the energy that exists between people when they feel seen, heard, and valued.

BRENÉ BROWN

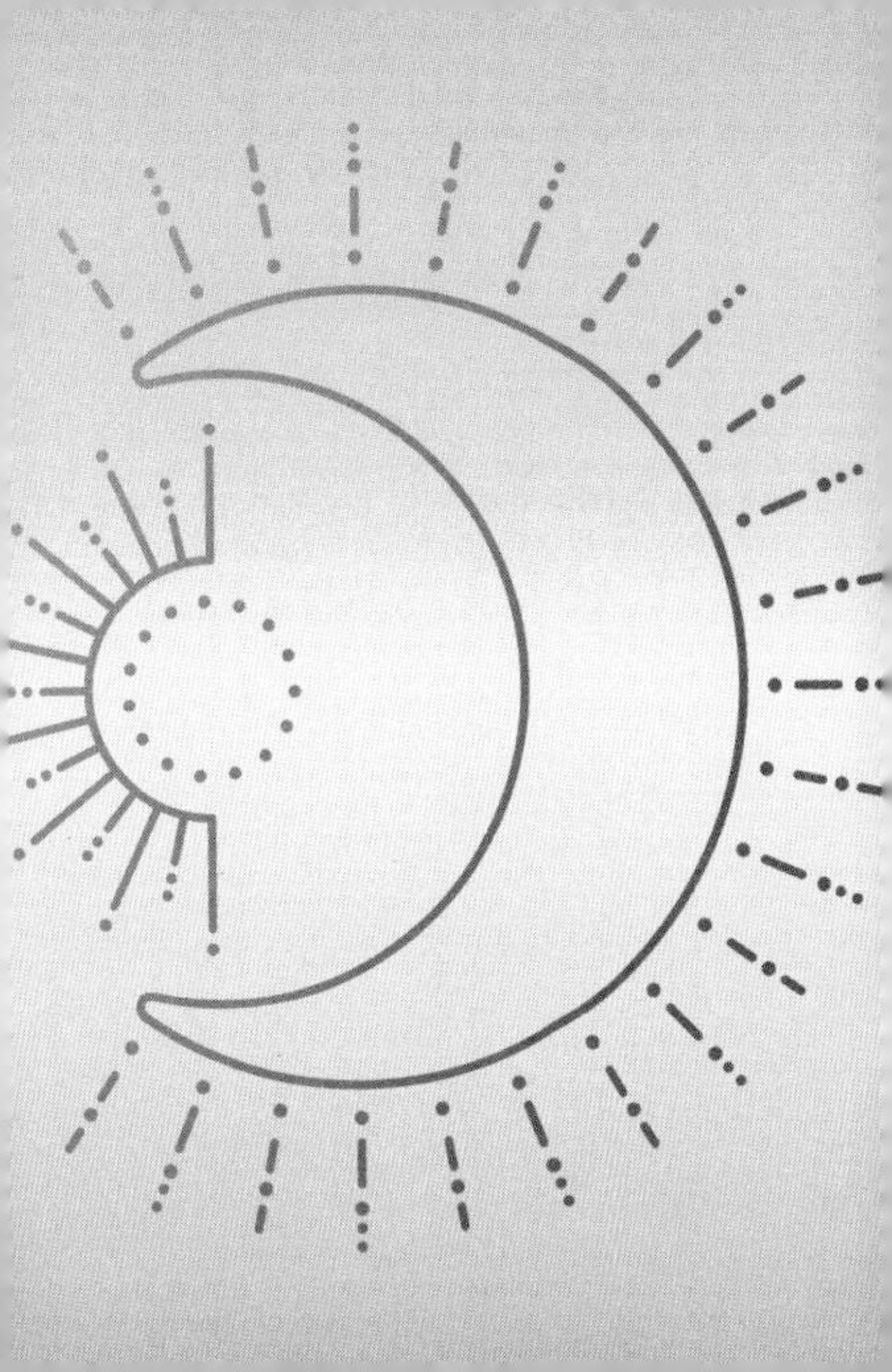

If you want to go QUICKLY, go alone. If you want to go far, go TOGETHER.

AFRICAN PROVERB

I AM A PART OF ALL THAT I HAVE MET.

ALFRED LORD TENNYSON

You win the
VICTORY
when you yield to
FRIENDS.

SOPHOCLES

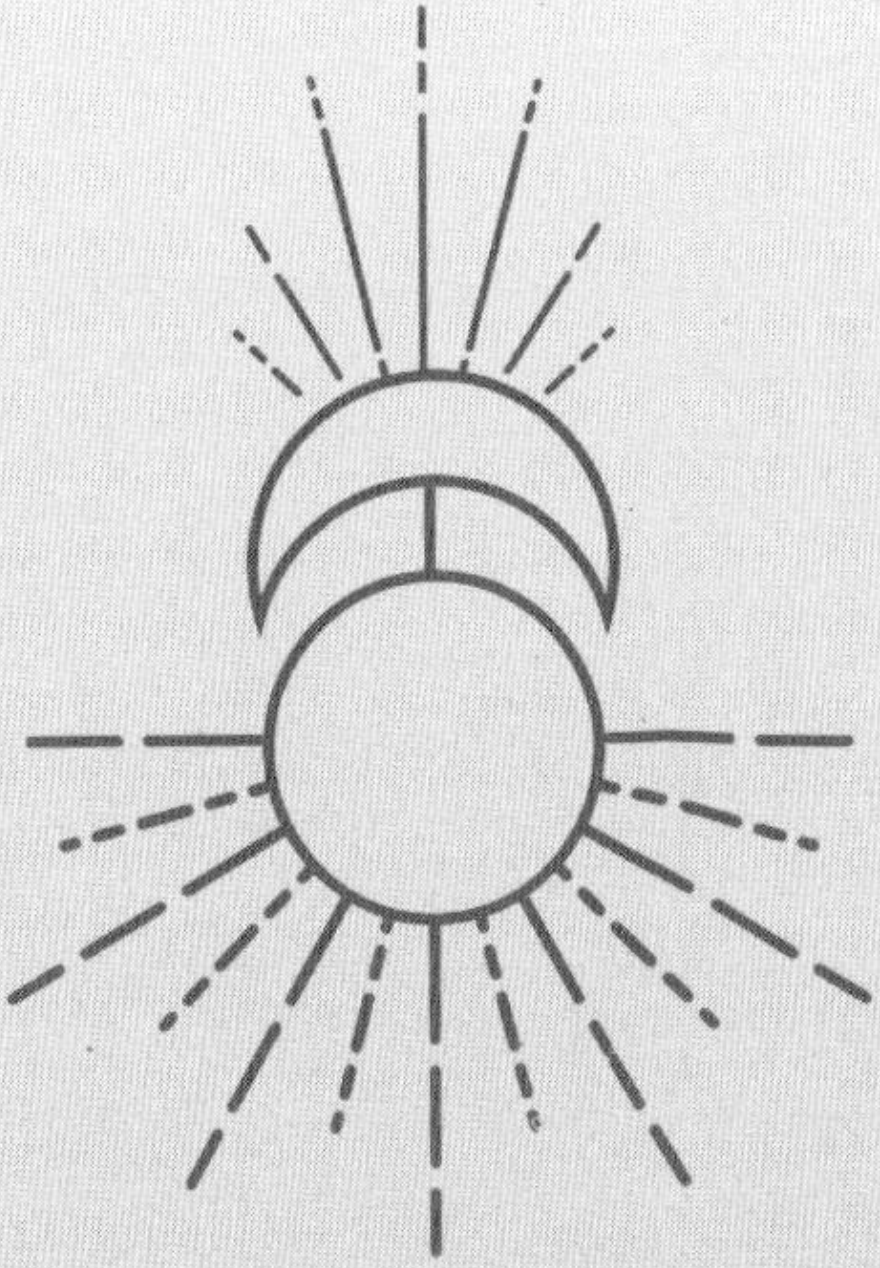

THE TRUE MEANING OF LIFE IS TO PLANT TREES UNDER WHOSE SHADE YOU DO NOT EXPECT TO SIT.

NELSON HENDERSON

Good company
and good discourse
are the very
sinews of virtue.

IZAAK WALTON

Empathy is being with someone and feeling with someone.

TAMARA LEVITT

The most
EXQUISITE
pleasure is giving
PLEASURE
to others.

JEAN DE LA BRUYÈRE

LIVE SO THAT YOUR FRIENDS CAN DEFEND YOU BUT NEVER HAVE TO.

ARNOLD H. GLASGOW

The golden way is to be friends with the world and to regard the whole human family as one.

MAHATMA GANDHI

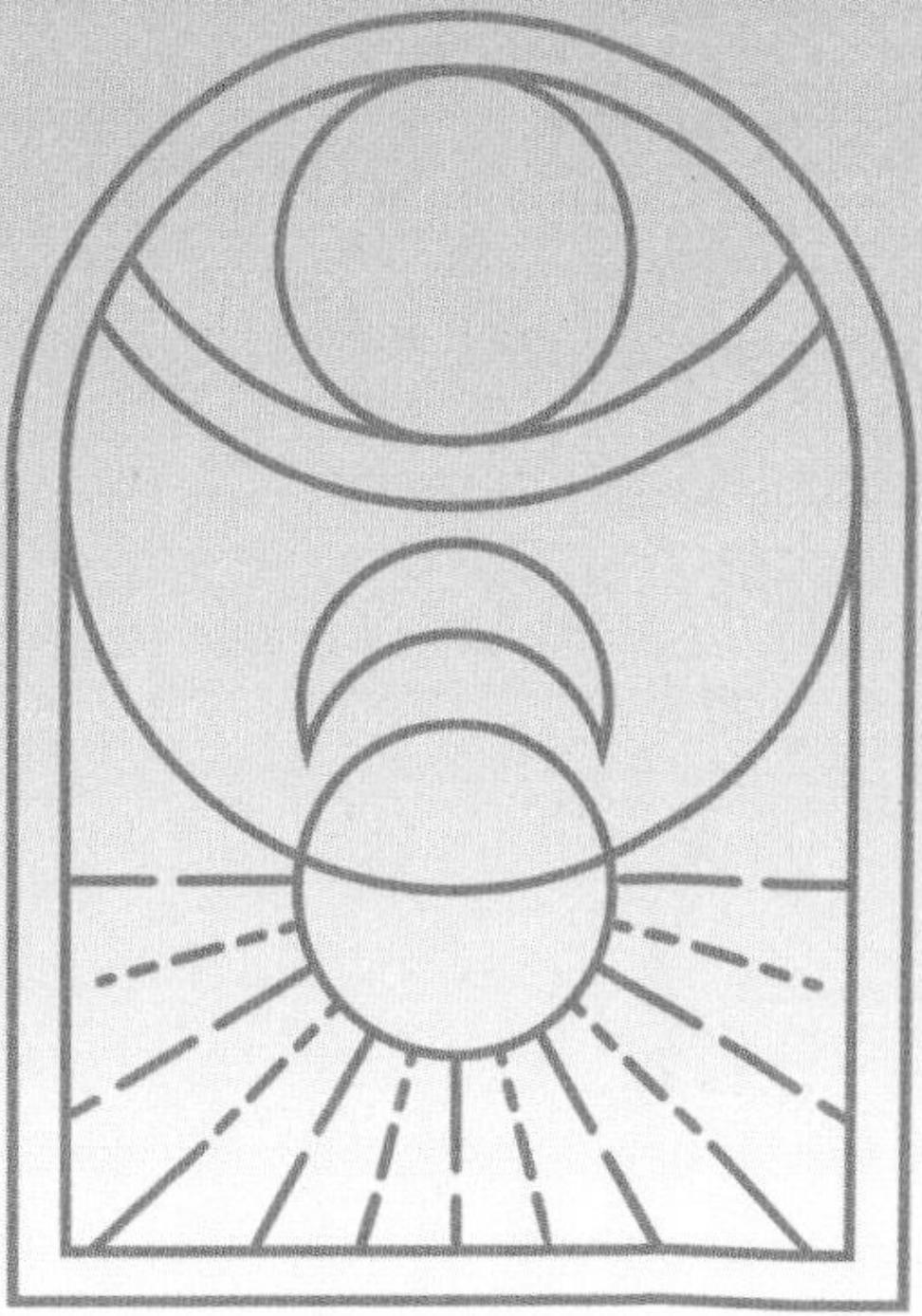

THE WORST SOLITUDE IS TO BE DESTITUTE OF SINCERE FRIENDSHIP.

FRANCIS BACON

Real unselfishness comes in sharing the interests of others.

GEORGE SANTAYANA

TO LIVE IS NOT TO LIVE FOR ONE'S SELF ALONE; LET US HELP ONE ANOTHER.

MENANDER

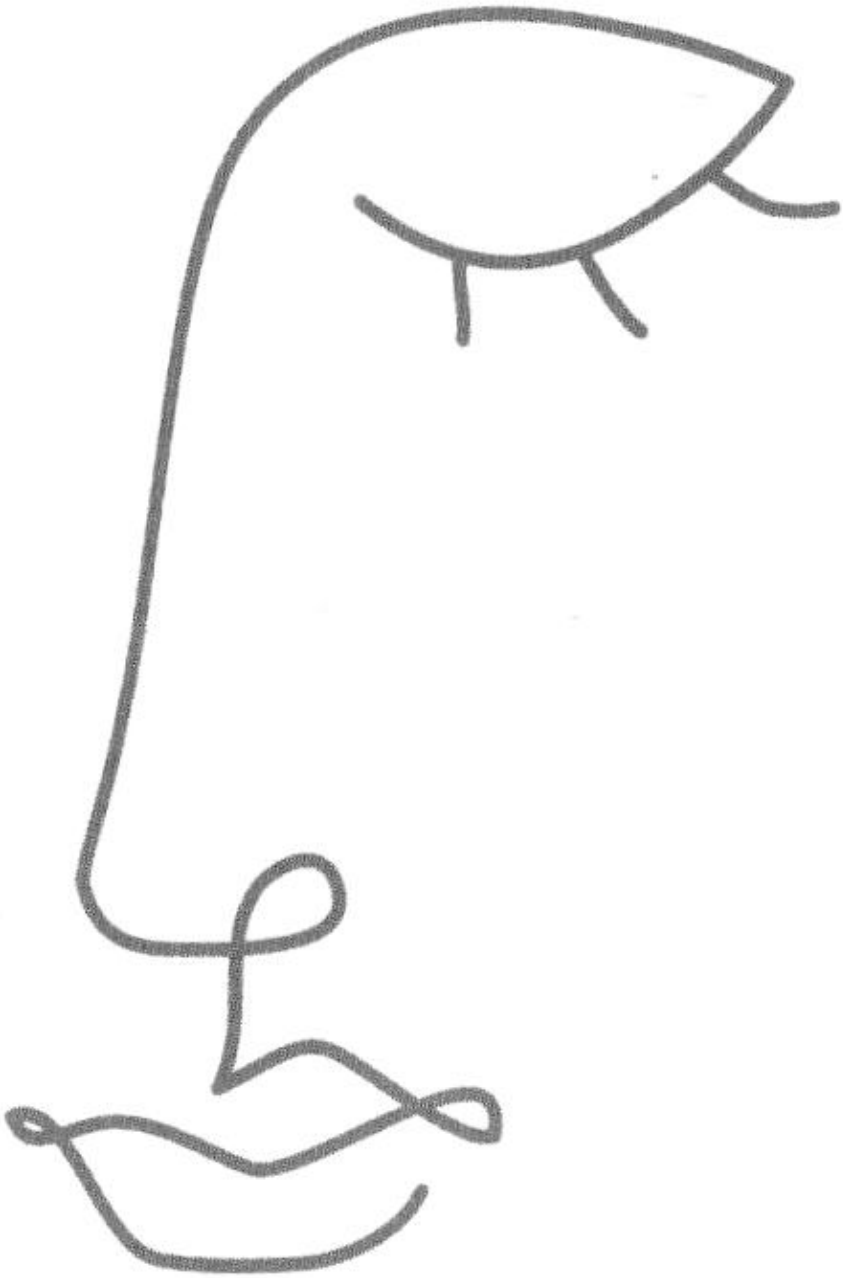

You can no more separate one life from another than you can separate a breeze from the wind.

MITCH ALBOM

Where there is great love, there are always miracles.

WILLA CATHER

If you want to be listened to, you should put in time listening.

MARGE PIERCY

The more complex
the network is,
the more complex
its pattern of
interconnections,
the more resilient
it will be.

FRITJOF CAPRA

The minute
we become an
integrated whole,
we look through
the same eyes
and we see a
whole different
world together.

AZIZAH AL-HIBRI

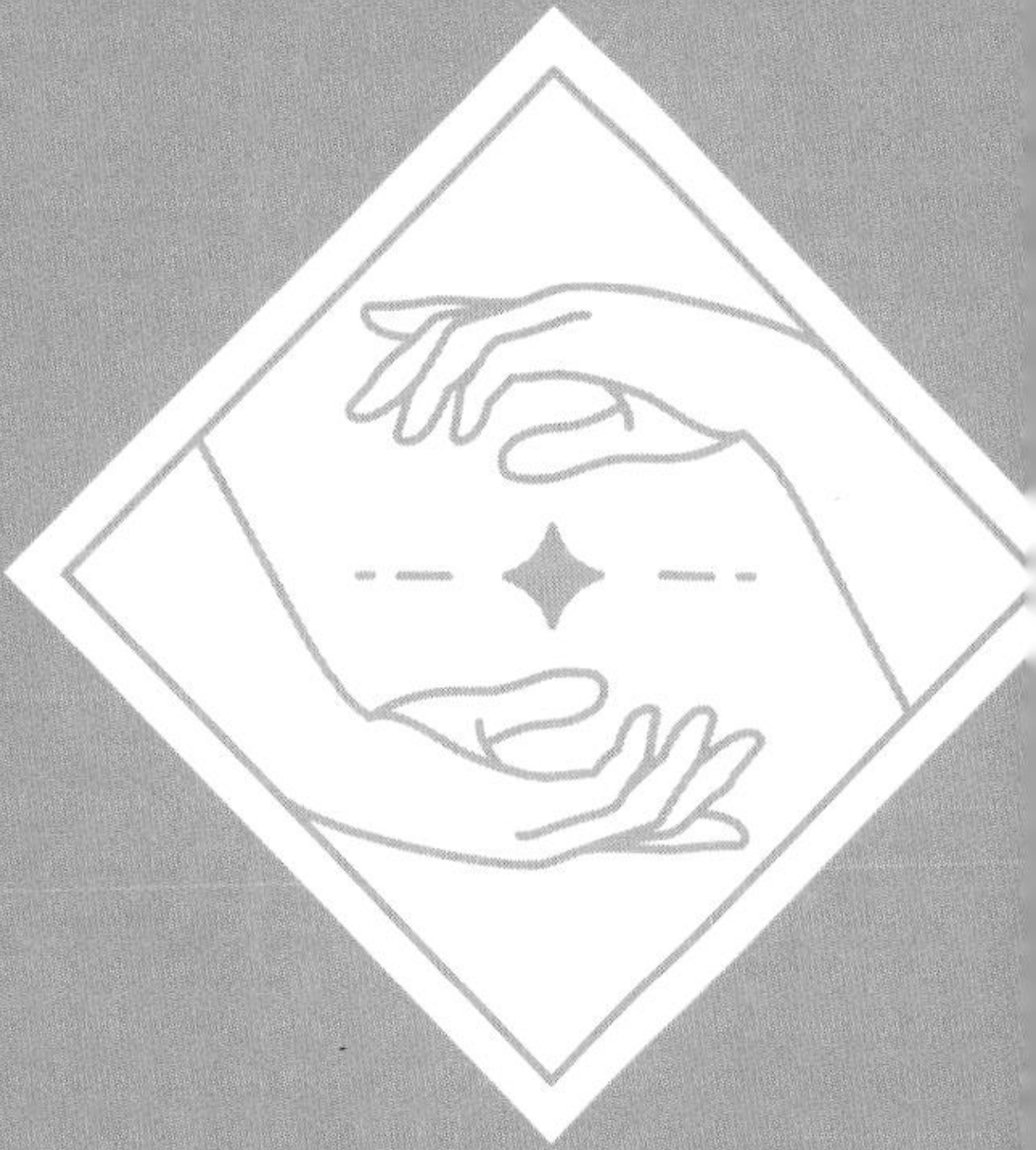

Habituated patterns create distance... openness and truth bring us closer together.

CHARLOTTE KASL

To give service
to a single heart
by a single act
is better than a
thousand heads
bowing in prayer.

MAHATMA GANDHI

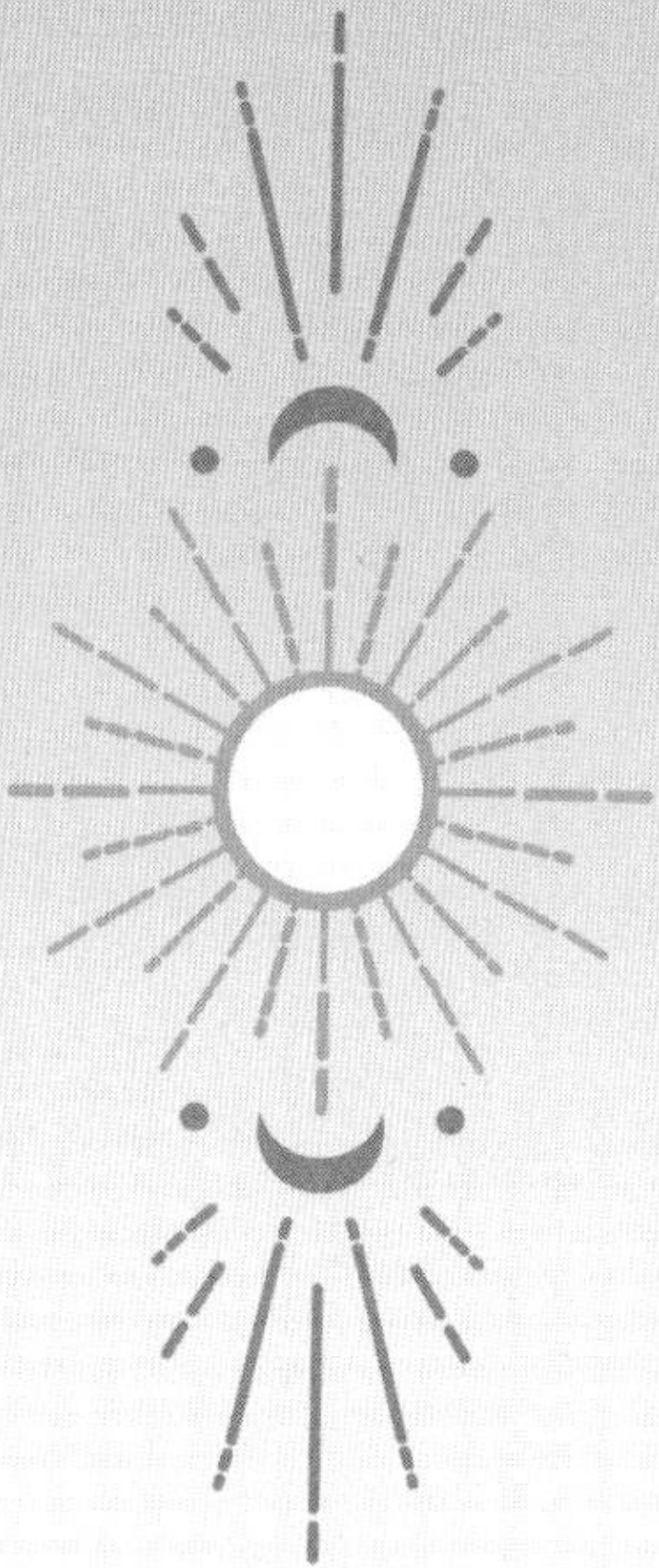

They may forget what you said, but they will never forget how you made them feel.

CARL W. BUEHNER

It is one of the most beautiful compensations of this life that no man can sincerely try to help another without helping himself.

RALPH WALDO EMERSON

One can bear grief, but it takes two to be glad.

ELBERT HUBBARD

OUR AFFECTIONS ARE OUR LIFE. WE LIVE BY THEM; THEY SUPPLY OUR WARMTH.

WILLIAM ELLERY CHANNING

Love lights more fires than hate extinguishes.

ELLA WHEELER WILCOX

We are all connected—to each other, biologically; to the earth, chemically; to the rest of the universe, atomically.

NEIL DEGRASSE TYSON

If you JUDGE people, you have no time to LOVE them.

MOTHER TERESA

AGE DOES NOT PROTECT YOU FROM LOVE, BUT LOVE, TO SOME EXTENT, PROTECTS YOU FROM AGE.

JEANNE MOREAU

We cannot live
only for ourselves.

HERMAN MELVILLE

WE CANNOT HOLD A TORCH TO LIGHT ANOTHER'S PATH WITHOUT BRIGHTENING OUR OWN.

BEN SWEETLAND

I LOVE, AND THE WORLD IS MINE!

FLORENCE EARLE COATES

The service we render others is the rent we pay for our room on earth.

WILFRED GRENFELL

EVERYTHING THAT LIVES, LIVES NOT ALONE, NOR FOR ITSELF.

WILLIAM BLAKE

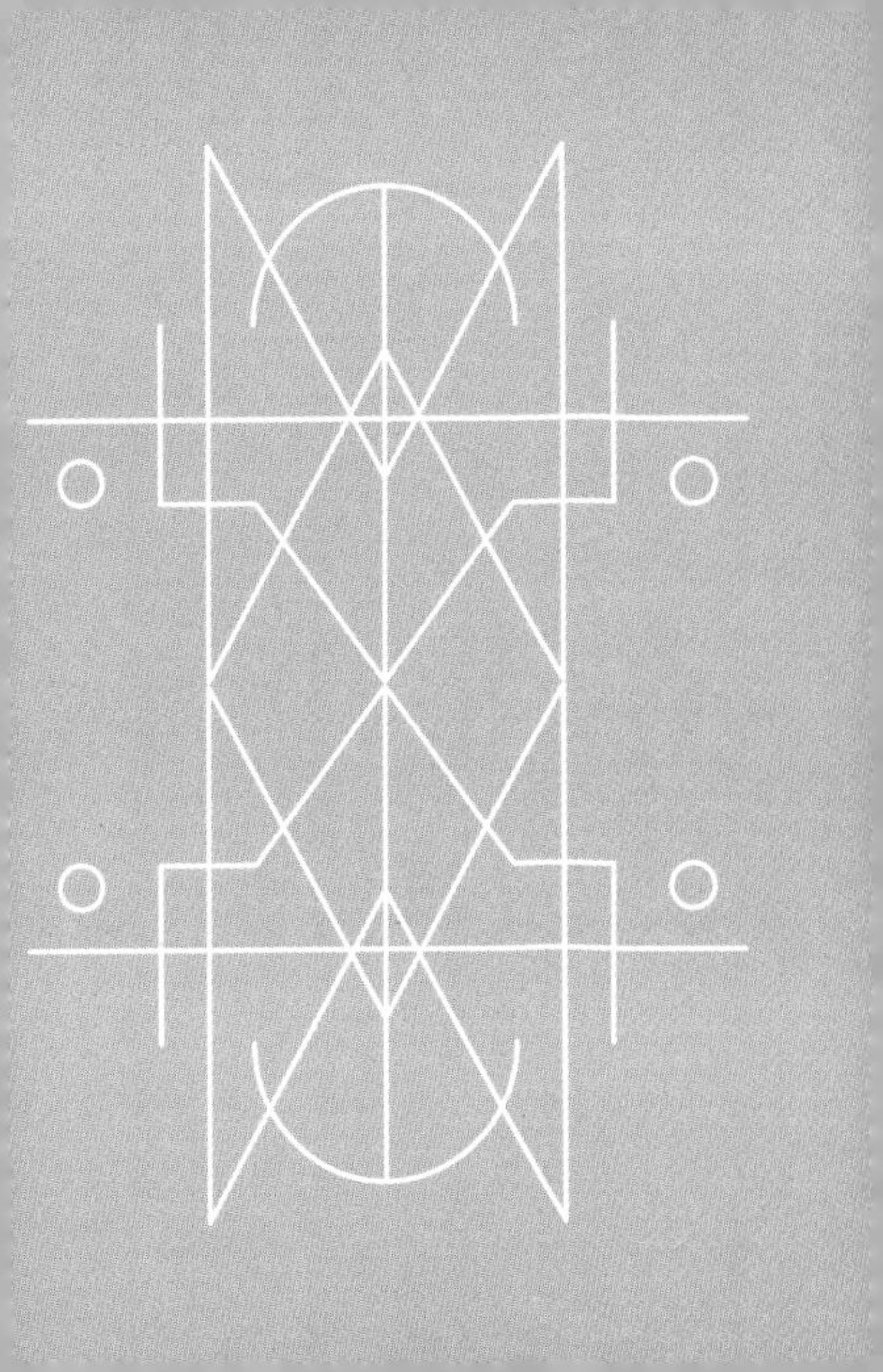

Real friendship is shown in times of trouble.

EURIPIDES

Affinities are rare. They come but a few times in a life. It is awful to risk losing one when it arrives.

FLORENCE H. WINTERBURN

The gift of paying attention is a fundamental key to transforming our relationships.

DEEPAK CHOPRA

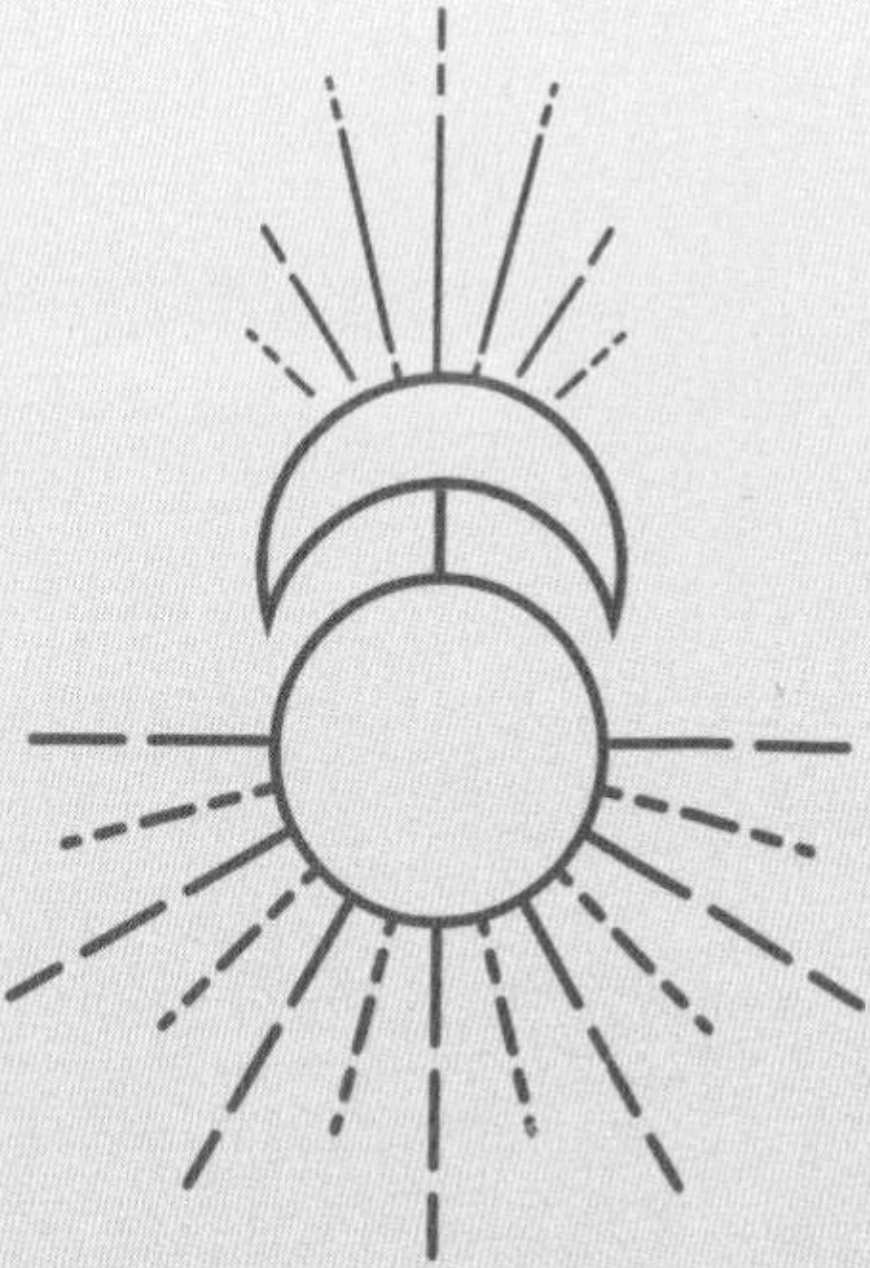

A bit of fragrance always clings to the hand that gives you roses.

CHINESE PROVERB

We are like islands in the sea, separate on the surface but connected in the deep.

WILLIAM JAMES

I believe that every human mind feels pleasure in doing good to another.

THOMAS JEFFERSON

If you understand,
and you show that
you understand,
you can love,
and the situation
will change.

THÍCH NHẤT HẠNH

We are members, one of another, so that you cannot injure or help your neighbor without injuring or helping yourself.

GEORGE BERNARD SHAW

NO ROAD IS LONG WITH GOOD COMPANY.

TURKISH PROVERB

Treat everyone you meet as if they were you.

DOUG DILLON

The greatness of a community is most accurately measured by the compassionate actions of its members.

CORETTA SCOTT KING

Life is partly what
we make it and
partly what is made
by the friends
we choose.

TENNESSEE WILLIAMS

The entire population of the universe, with one trifling exception, is composed of others.

JOHN ANDREW HOLMES

It is enough that
I am of value to
somebody today.

HUGH PRATHER

Never doubt that a small group of thoughtful, committed citizens can change the world; indeed, it's the only thing that ever has.

MARGARET MEAD

THERE IS NOTHING ON THIS EARTH MORE TO BE PRIZED THAN TRUE FRIENDSHIP.

SAINT THOMAS AQUINAS

Hold a true friend with both your hands.

NIGERIAN PROVERB

Good communication is as stimulating as black coffee, and just as hard to sleep after.

ANNE MORROW LINDBERGH

PLEASURE IS A NECESSARY RECIPROCAL. NO ONE FEELS WHO DOES NOT AT THE SAME TIME GIVE IT.

LORD CHESTERFIELD

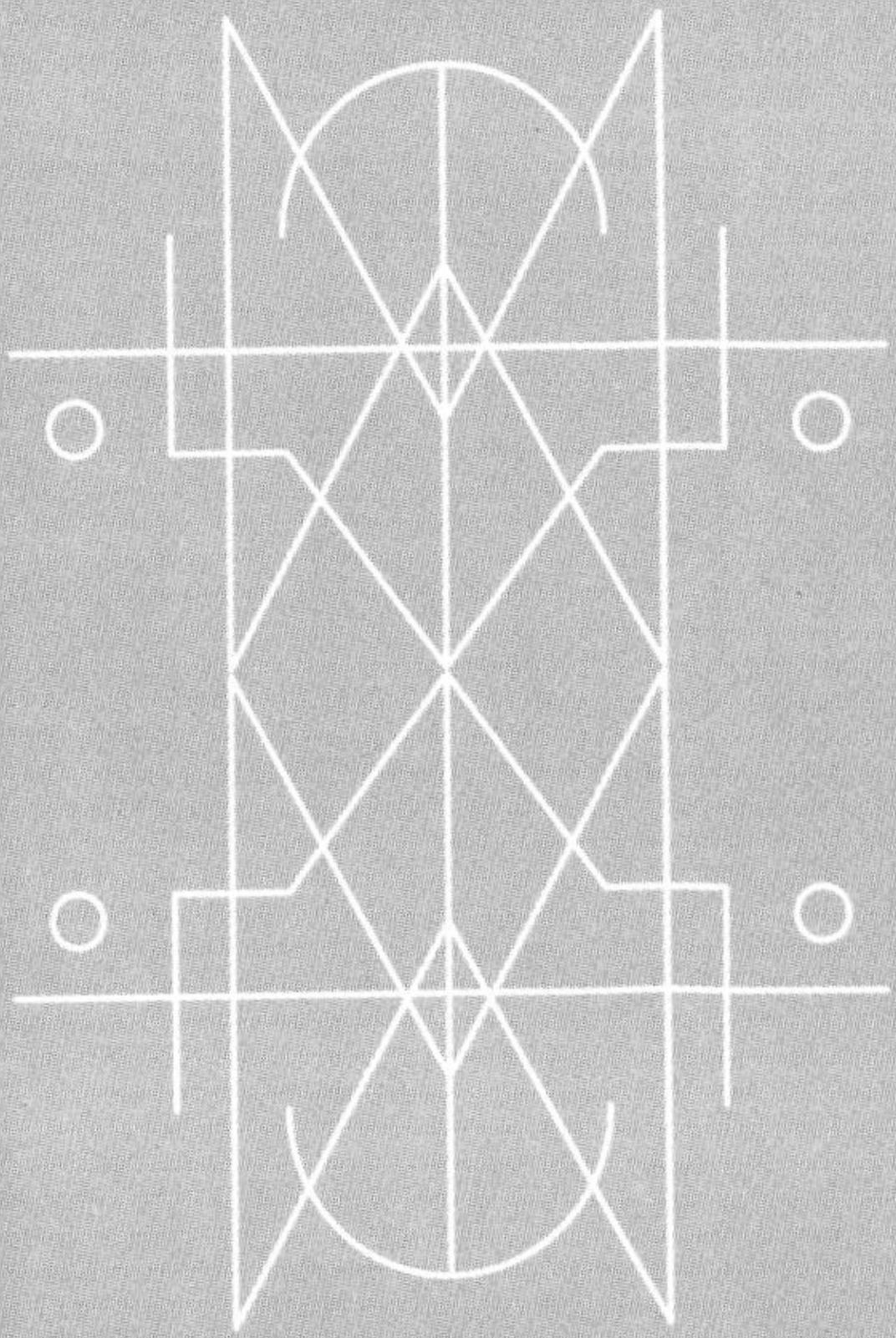

The fate of this man
or that man was
less than a drop,
although it was a
sparkling one, in the
great blue motion
of the sunlit sea.

T.H. WHITE

No man can be happy without a friend, nor be sure of his friend until he is unhappy.

THOMAS FULLER

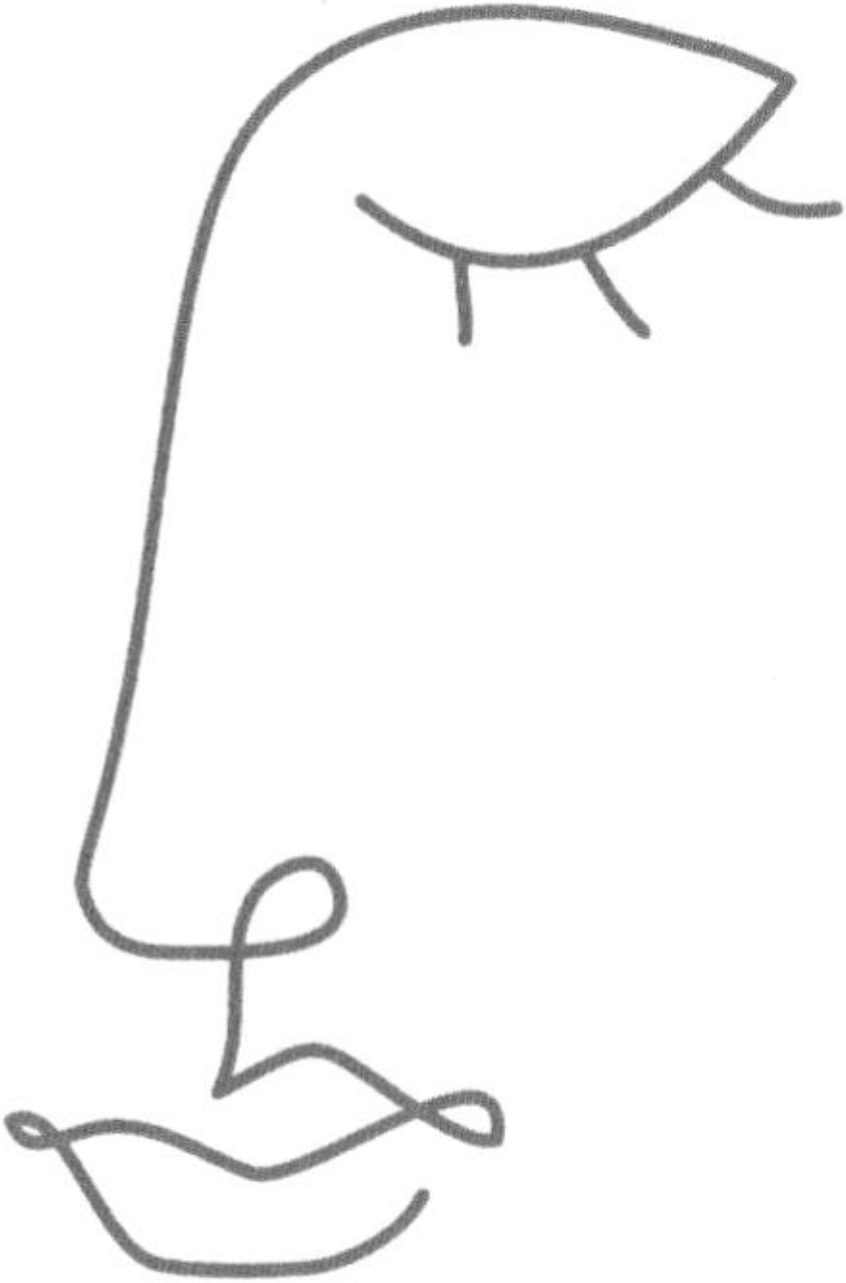

The smile is the shortest distance between two persons.

VICTOR BORGE

A man wrapped up in himself makes a very small bundle.

BENJAMIN FRANKLIN

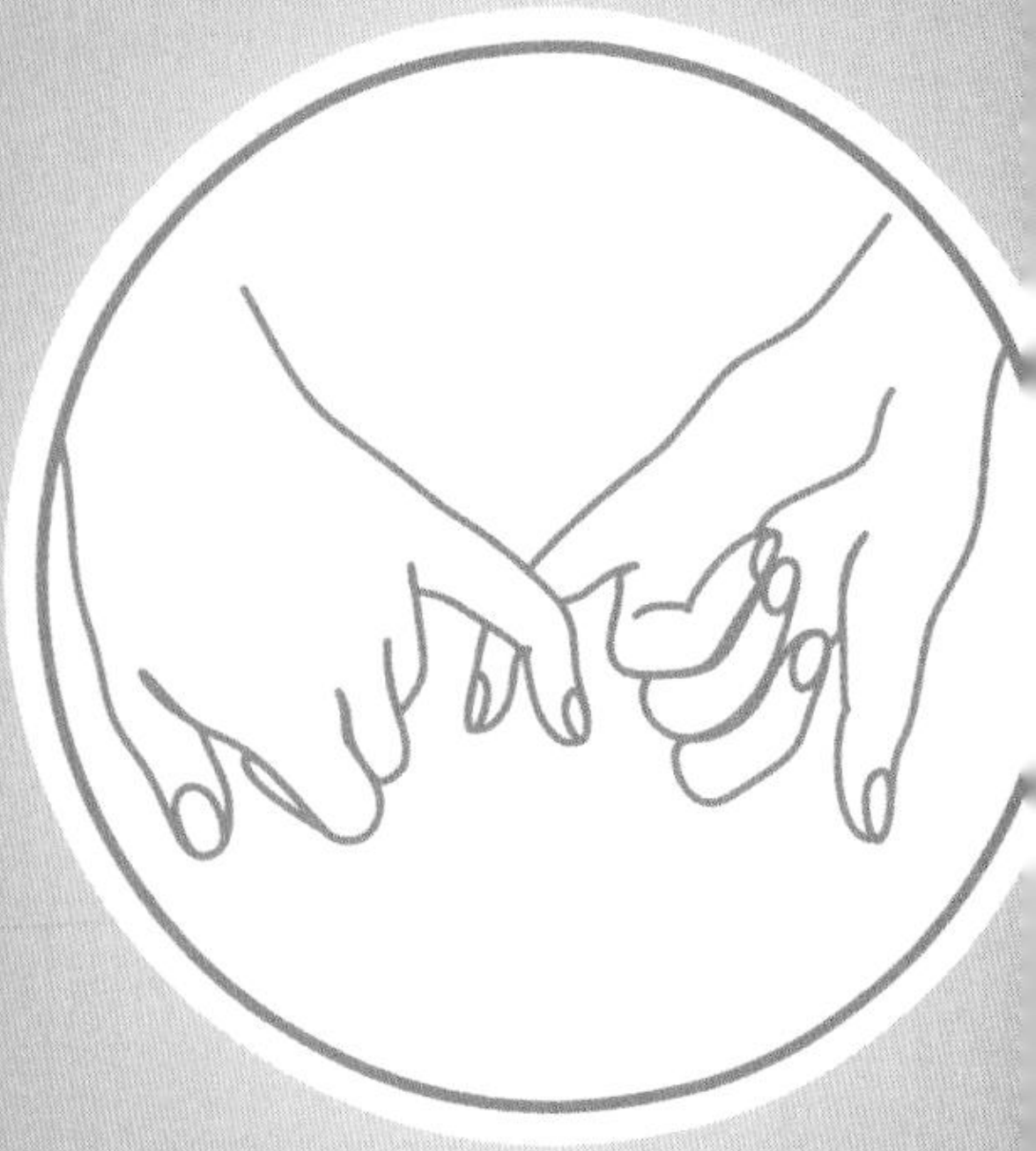

One of the deep secrets of life is that all that is really worth doing is what we do for others.

LEWIS CARROLL

I cannot concentrate all my friendship on any single one of my friends because no one is complete enough in himself.

ANAÏS NIN

You don't get HARMONY when everyone sings the same NOTE.

DOUG FLOYD

To be capable of steady friendship or lasting love are the two greatest proofs, not only of goodness of heart but of strength of mind.

WILLIAM HAZLITT

No man is an island,
entire of itself
every man is a piece
of the continent, a
part of the main.

JOHN DONNE

The best way to find out if you can trust somebody is to trust them.

ERNEST HEMINGWAY

GENEROSITY
gives assistance
rather than
ADVICE.

MARQUIS DE
VAUVENARGUES

LOVE IS THE ONLY THING WE CAN CARRY WITH US WHEN WE GO, AND IT MAKES THE END SO EASY.

LOUISA MAY ALCOTT

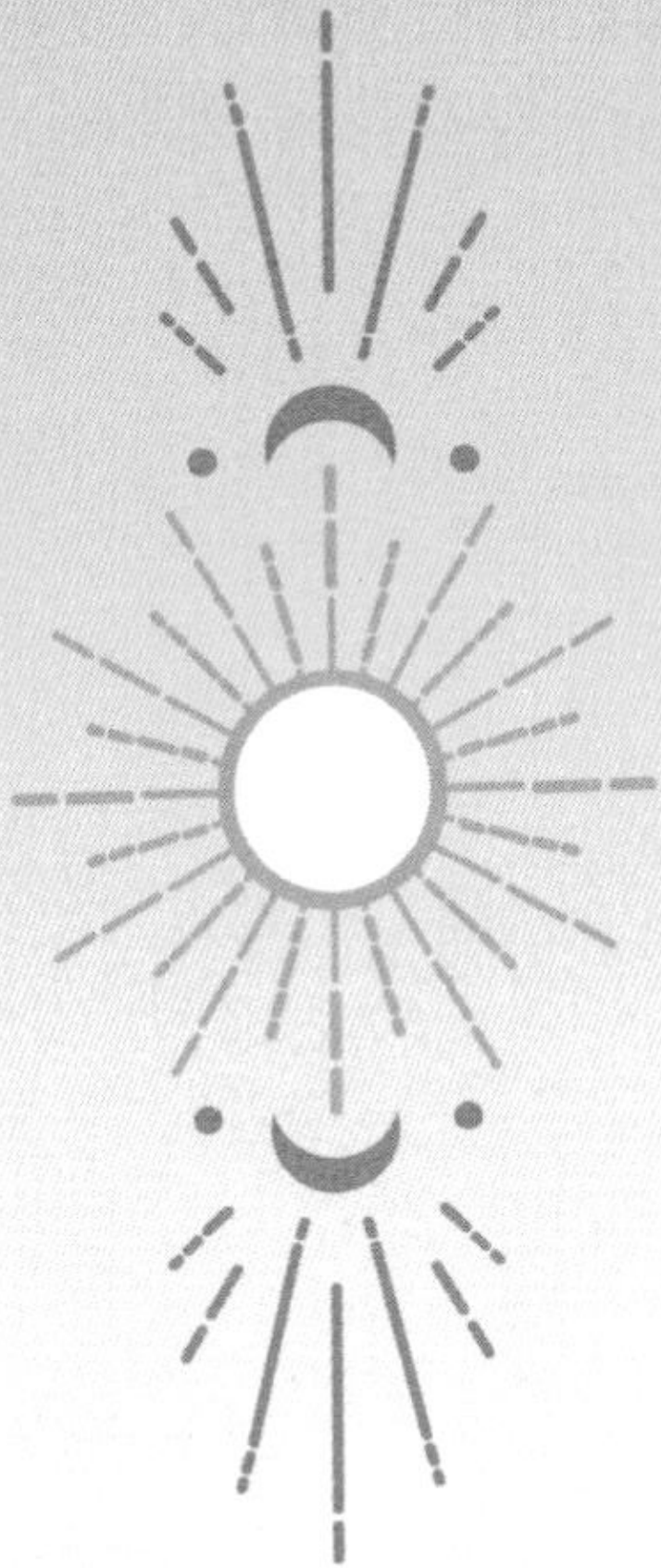

I alone cannot change the world, but I can cast a stone across the waters to create many ripples.

MOTHER TERESA

PROVISION
for others is a
FUNDAMENTAL
responsibility of
HUMAN LIFE.

WOODROW WILSON

When you cease to make a contribution, you begin to die.

ELEANOR ROOSEVELT

THE BEAUTY YOU SEE IN ME IS A REFLECTION OF YOU.

RUMI

A DREAM
YOU DREAM
ALONE IS ONLY
A DREAM.
A DREAM
YOU DREAM
TOGETHER
IS REALITY.

YOKO ONO

The entire sum of existence is the magic of being needed by just one person.

VII PUTNAM

BE KIND
WHENEVER
POSSIBLE.
IT IS ALWAYS
POSSIBLE.

DALAI LAMA XIV

One of the most important things you can do on this earth is to let people know they are not alone.

SHANNON L. ALDER

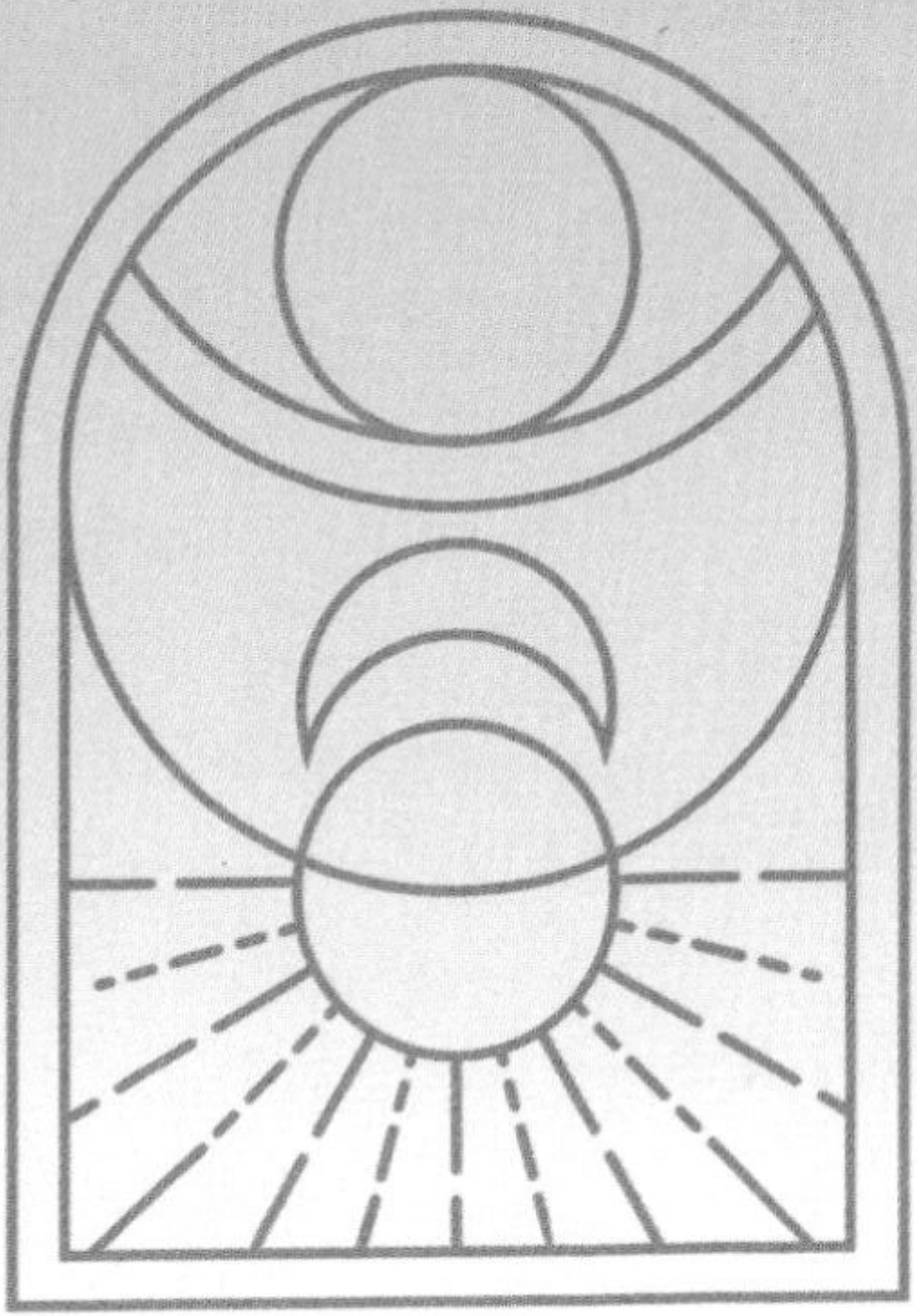

Kindness can become its own motive. We are made kind by being kind.

ERIC HOFFER

Happiness never decreases by being shared.

BUKKYO DENDO KYOKAI

Wear a smile and have friends; wear a scowl and have wrinkles.

GEORGE ELIOT

What can you do to promote world peace? Go home and love your family.

MOTHER TERESA

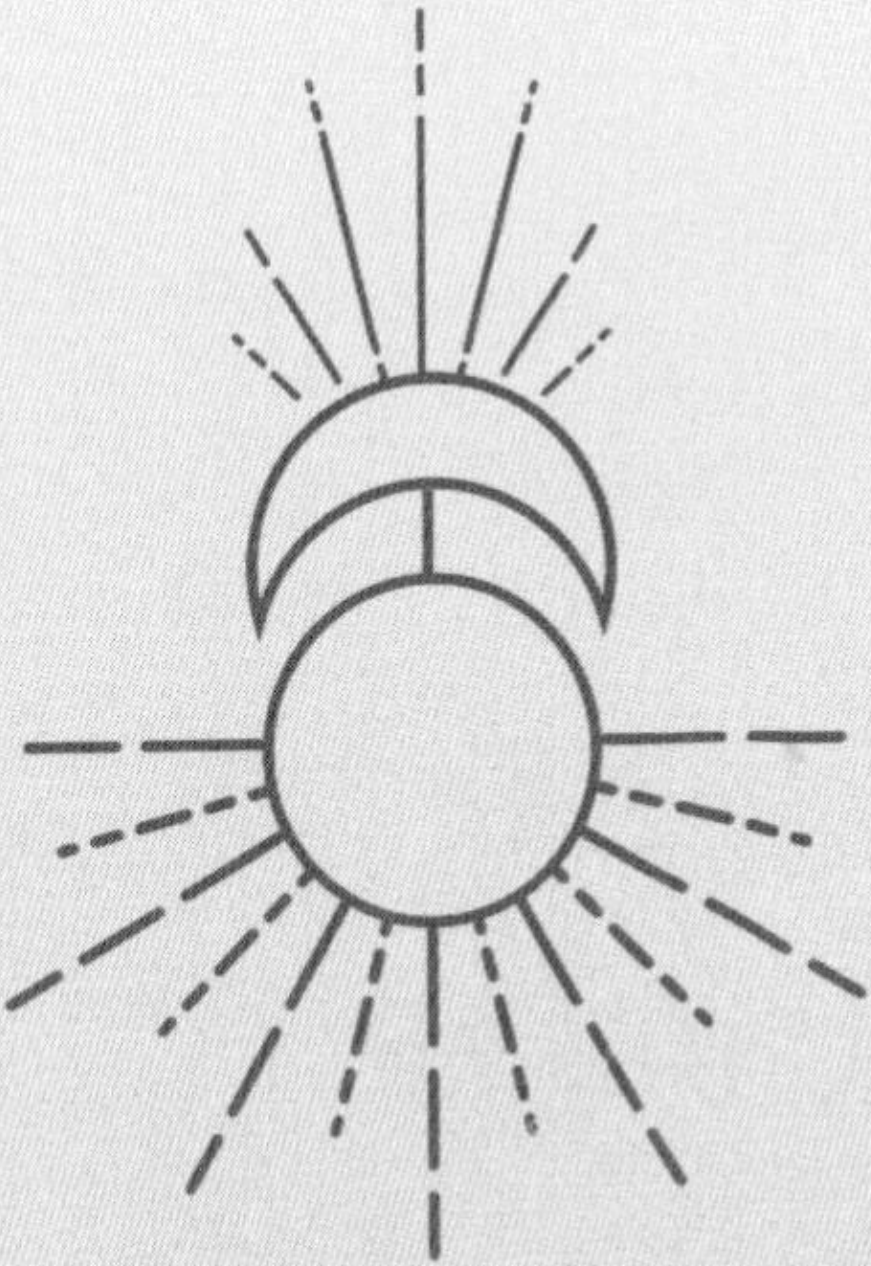

Community, above all, is bigger than individuals; we are something much more than individuals when we are part of a community.

TONY BLACKSHAW

THE MEASURE OF LOVE IS TO LOVE WITHOUT MEASURE.

SAINT FRANCIS DE SALES

Even the technology that promises to unite us divides us.

DAN BROWN

ALL WHO JOY
WOULD WIN
MUST SHARE IT—
HAPPINESS WAS
BORN A TWIN.

LORD BYRON

WE WERE BORN TO UNITE WITH OUR FELLOW MEN AND TO JOIN IN COMMUNITY WITH THE HUMAN RACE.

MARCUS TULLIUS CICERO

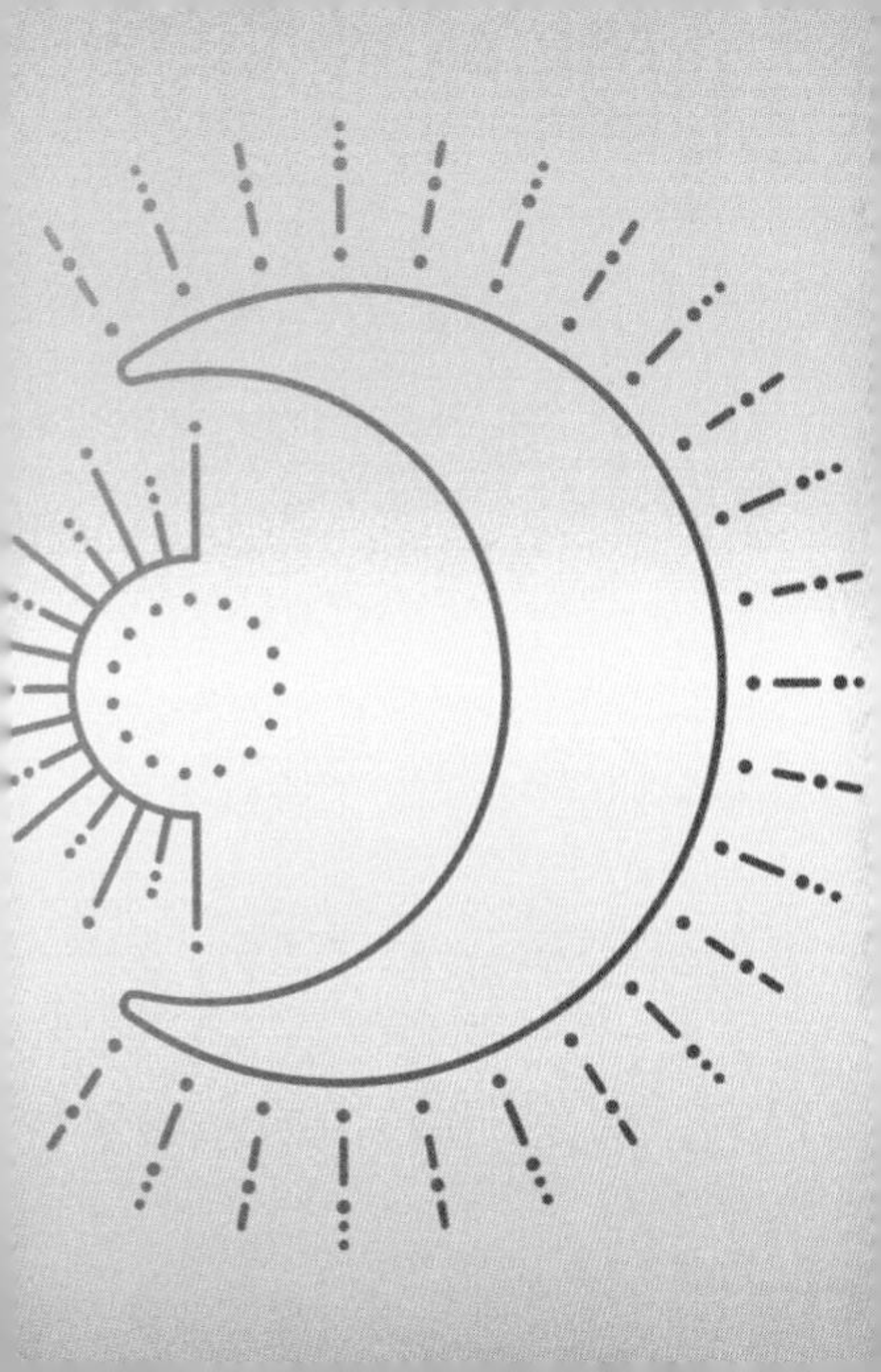

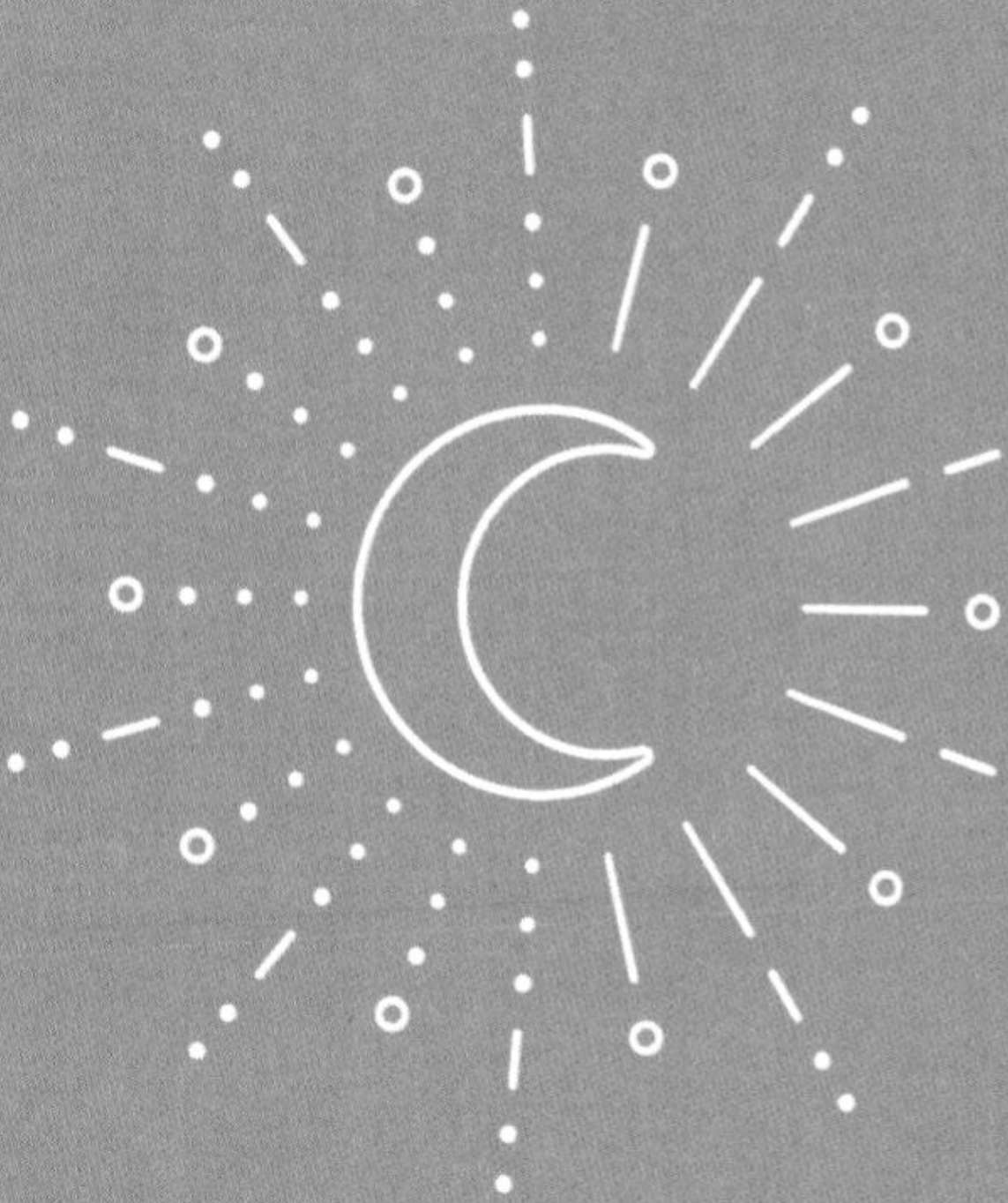

We all live with the objective of being happy; our lives are all different, and yet the same.

ANNE FRANK

A good friend is my nearest relation.

THOMAS FULLER

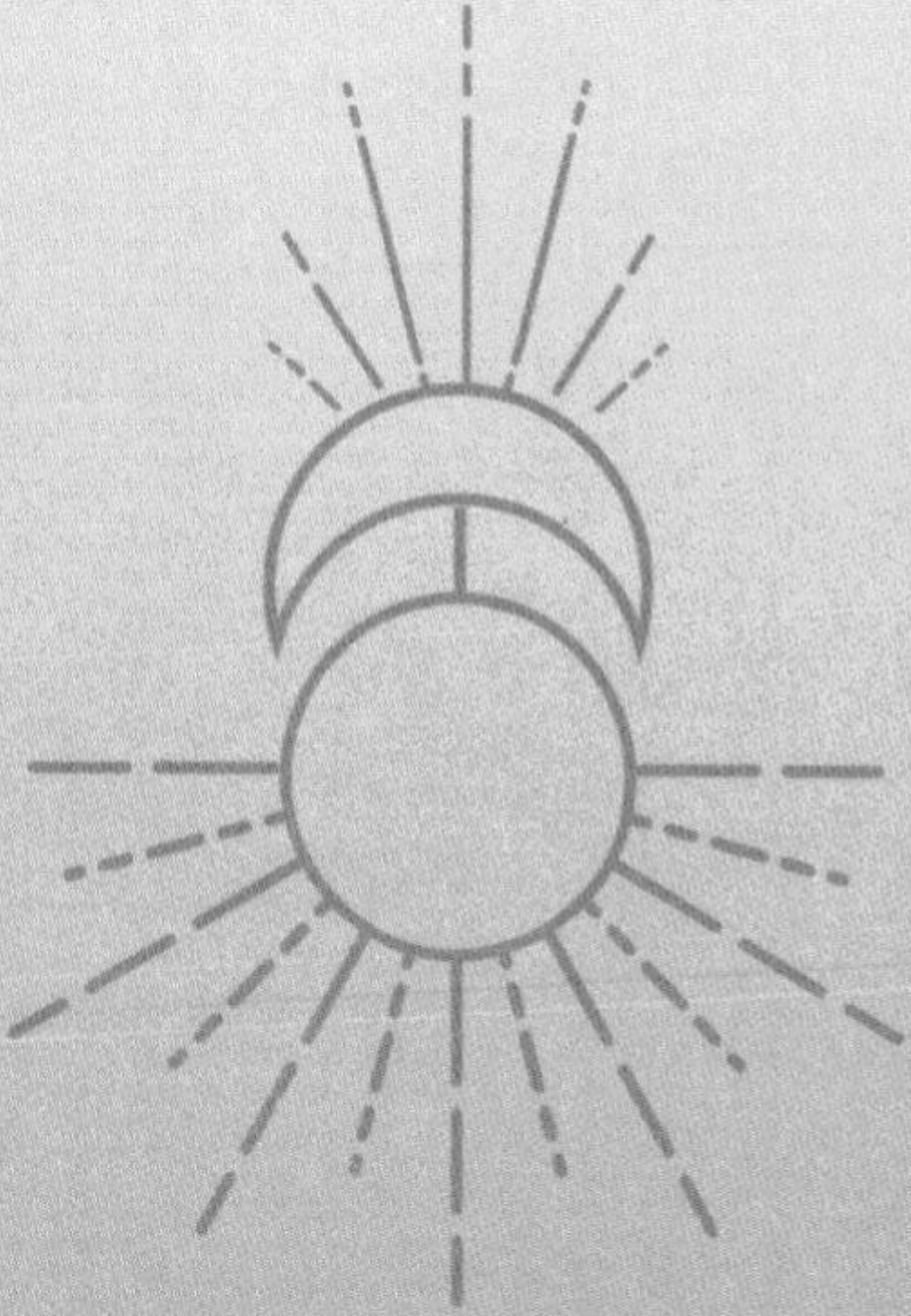

The more we genuinely care about others, the greater our own happiness and inner peace.

ALLAN LOKOS

FORGIVING THOSE WHO HURT US IS THE KEY TO PERSONAL PEACE.

ULYSSES G. WEATHERLY

When we get too caught up in the busyness of the world, we lose connection with one another—and ourselves.

JACK KORNFIELD

Love and compassion are necessities, not luxuries. Without them humanity cannot survive.

DALAI LAMA XIV

LOVE cannot live where there is no TRUST.

EDITH HAMILTON

COMPASSION IS THE BASIS OF ALL MORALITY.

ARTHUR SCHOPENHAUER

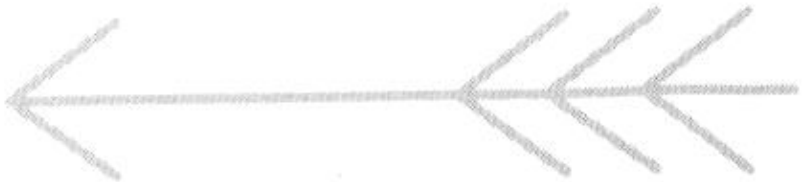

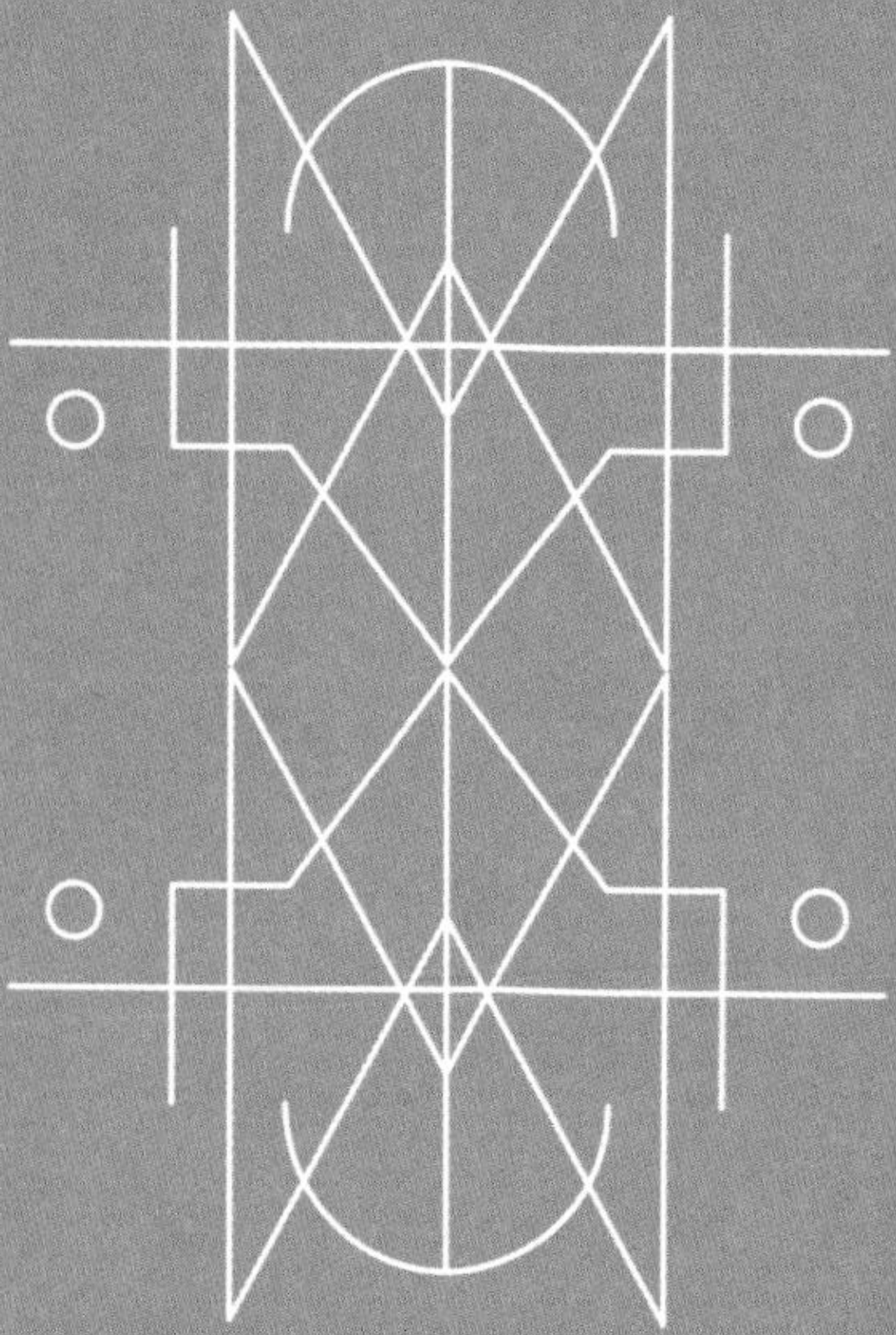

Every person is defined by the communities she belongs to.

ORSON SCOTT CARD

Interdependence is and ought to be as much the ideal of man as self-sufficiency.

MAHATMA GANDHI

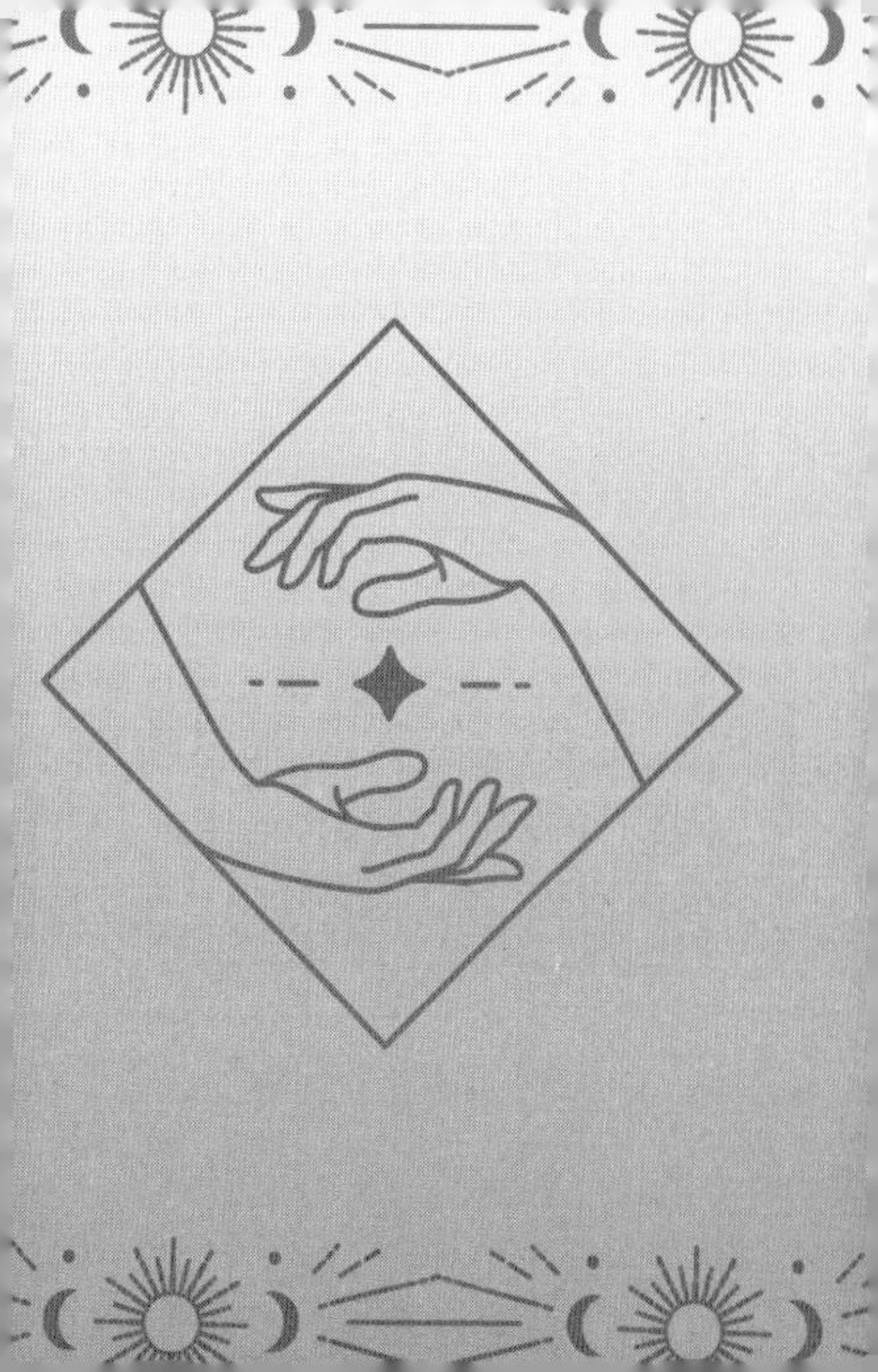

HAVE FRIENDS.
'TIS A SECOND
EXISTENCE.

BALTASAR GRACIÁN

YOU CANNOT BE LONELY IF YOU LIKE THE PERSON YOU ARE ALONE WITH.

WAYNE DYER

The supreme happiness of life is the conviction that we are loved.

VICTOR HUGO

SINCE YOU CANNOT DO GOOD TO ALL, YOU ARE TO PAY SPECIAL ATTENTION TO THOSE WHO, BY THE ACCIDENTS OF TIME, OR PLACE, OR

CIRCUMSTANCES, ARE BROUGHT INTO CLOSER CONNECTION WITH YOU.

AUGUSTINE OF HIPPO

He that walketh
with wise men
shall be wise.

SOLOMON

Only a life lived for others is a life worthwhile.

ALBERT EINSTEIN

HELP YOUR BROTHER'S BOAT ACROSS AND YOUR OWN WILL REACH THE SHORE.

HINDU PROVERB

Eventually everything connects—people, ideas, objects. The quality of the connections is the key to quality per se.

CHARLES EAMES

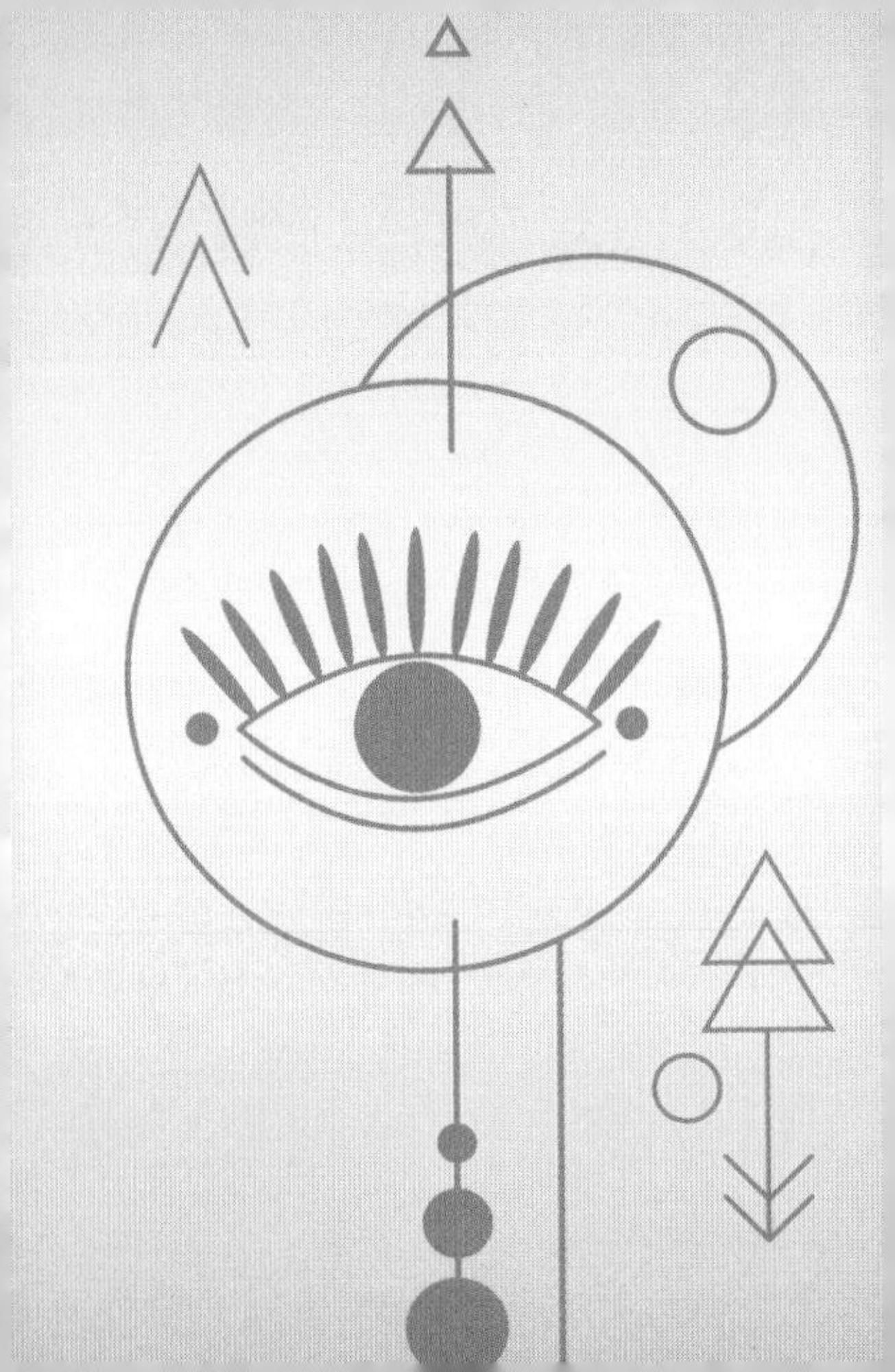

INSTINCT TEACHES US TO LOOK FOR HAPPINESS OUTSIDE OURSELVES.

BLAISE PASCAL

If we had no regard for others' feelings or fortune, we would grow cold and indifferent to life itself.

GEORGE MATTHEW ADAMS

ALONE, WE CAN DO SO LITTLE; TOGETHER, WE CAN DO SO MUCH.

HELEN KELLER

Adversity not only draws people together but brings forth that beautiful inward friendship.

SØREN KIERKEGAARD

The true way to soften one's troubles is to solace those of others.

MADAME DE MAINTENON

BE BRAVE ENOUGH TO ACCEPT THE HELP OF OTHERS.

MELBA COLGROVE

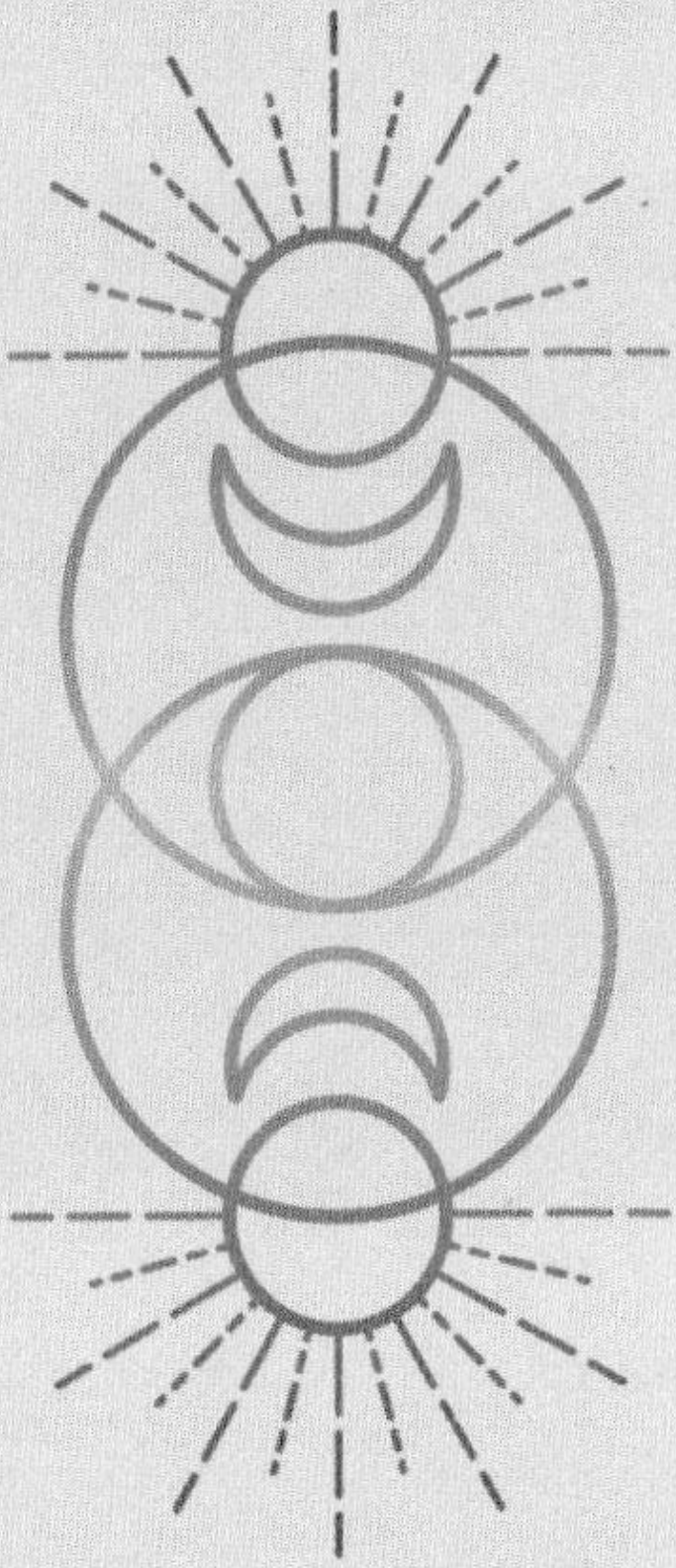

Set your life on fire. Seek those who fan your flames.

RUMI

TO BE
SOCIAL
IS TO BE
FORGIVING.

ROBERT FROST

Friendship improves happiness and abates misery, by the doubling of our joy and the dividing of our grief.

MARCUS TULLIUS CICERO

ONE'S FRIENDS ARE THAT PART OF THE HUMAN RACE WITH WHICH ONE CAN BE HUMAN.

GEORGE SANTAYANA

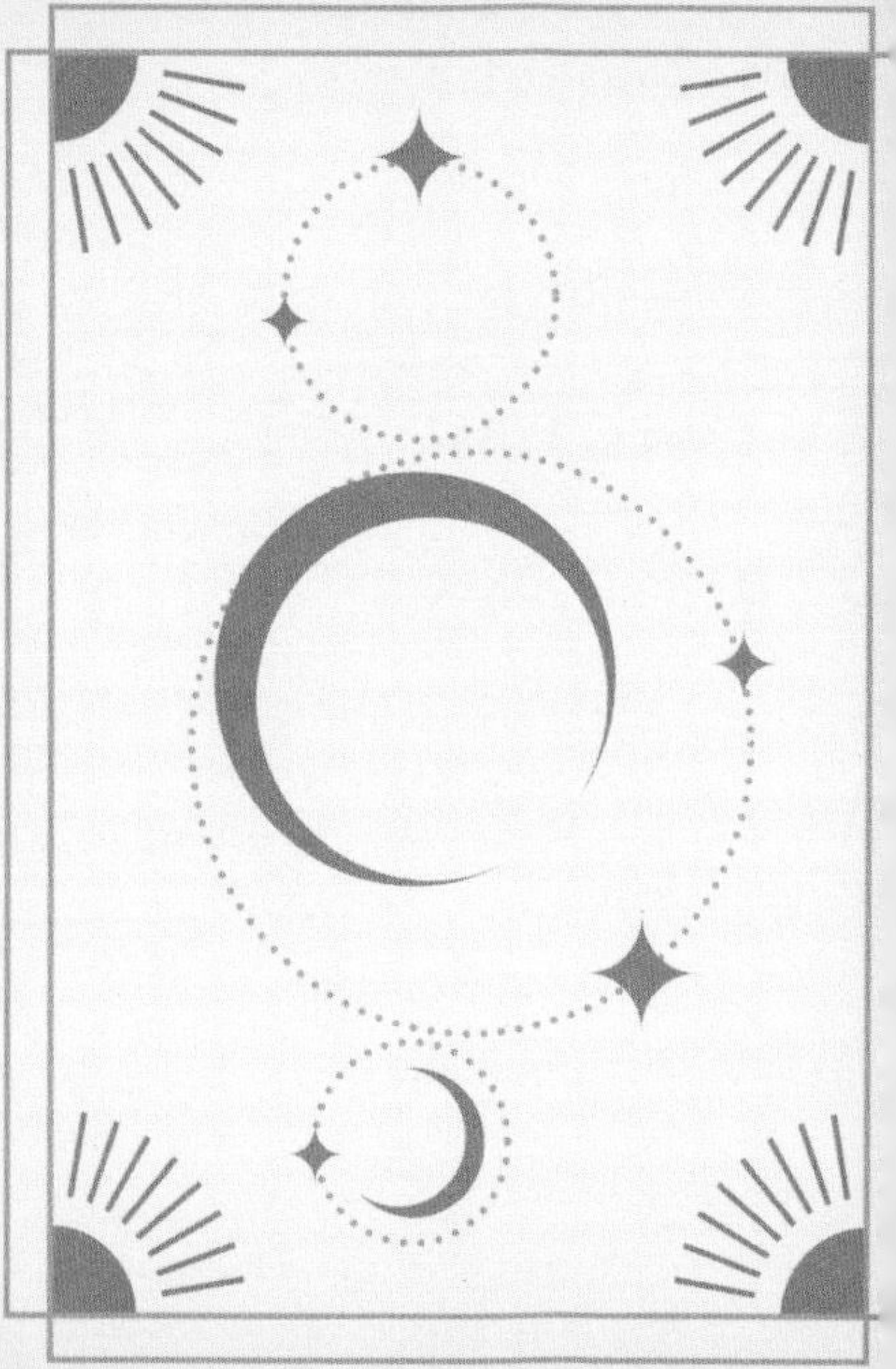

THERE IS NO HOPE OR JOY EXCEPT IN HUMAN RELATIONS.

ANTOINE DE SAINT-EXUPÉRY

INVISIBLE threads are the strongest ties.

FRIEDRICH NIETZSCHE

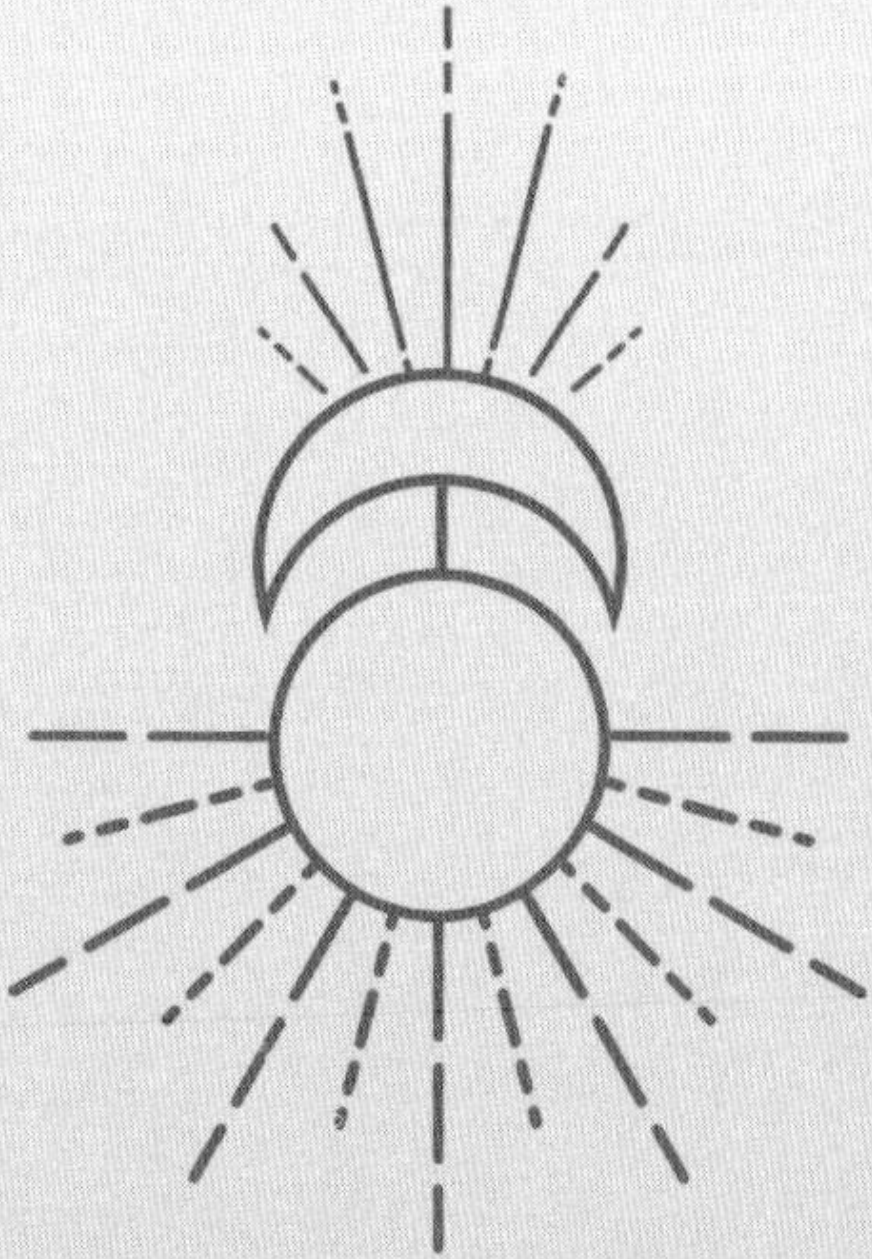

HEALING
yourself is
connected
with healing
OTHERS.

YOKO ONO

The habit of being uniformly considerate toward others will bring increased happiness to you.

GRENVILLE KLEISER

Society is no COMFORT to one not sociable.

WILLIAM SHAKESPEARE

THE BEST TIME TO MAKE FRIENDS IS BEFORE YOU NEED THEM.

ETHEL BARRYMORE

We all of us need assistance. Those who sustain others themselves want to be sustained.

MAURICE D'HULST

Communication is merely an exchange of information, but connection is an exchange of our humanity.

SEAN STEPHENSON

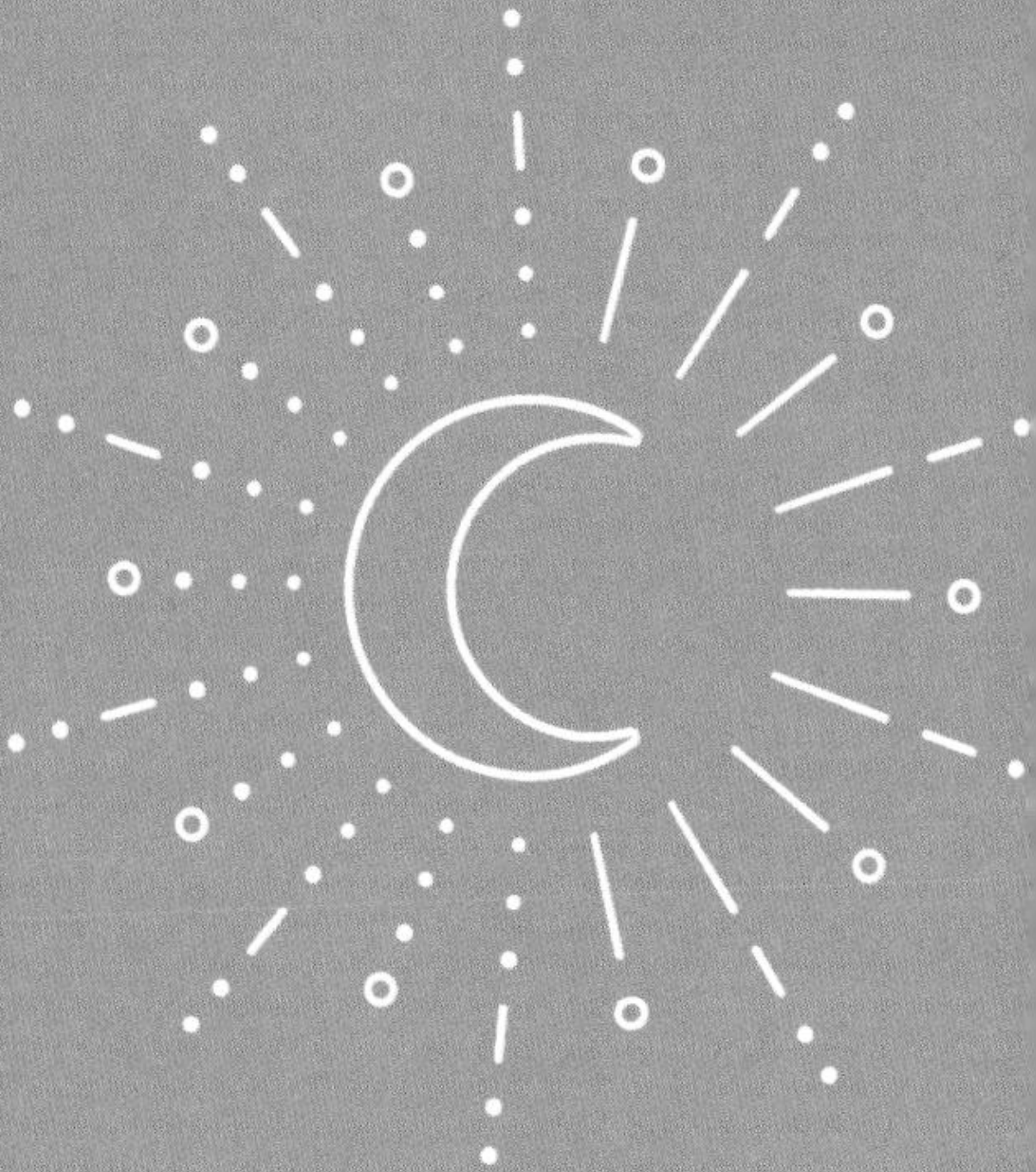

'Tis the privilege of friendship to talk nonsense and have her nonsense respected.

CHARLES LAMB

When we try to pick out anything by itself, we find it hitched to everything else in the Universe.

JOHN MUIR

People seldom improve when they have no other model but themselves to copy after.

OLIVER GOLDSMITH

A FRIEND MAY WELL BE RECKONED THE MASTERPIECE OF NATURE.

RALPH WALDO EMERSON

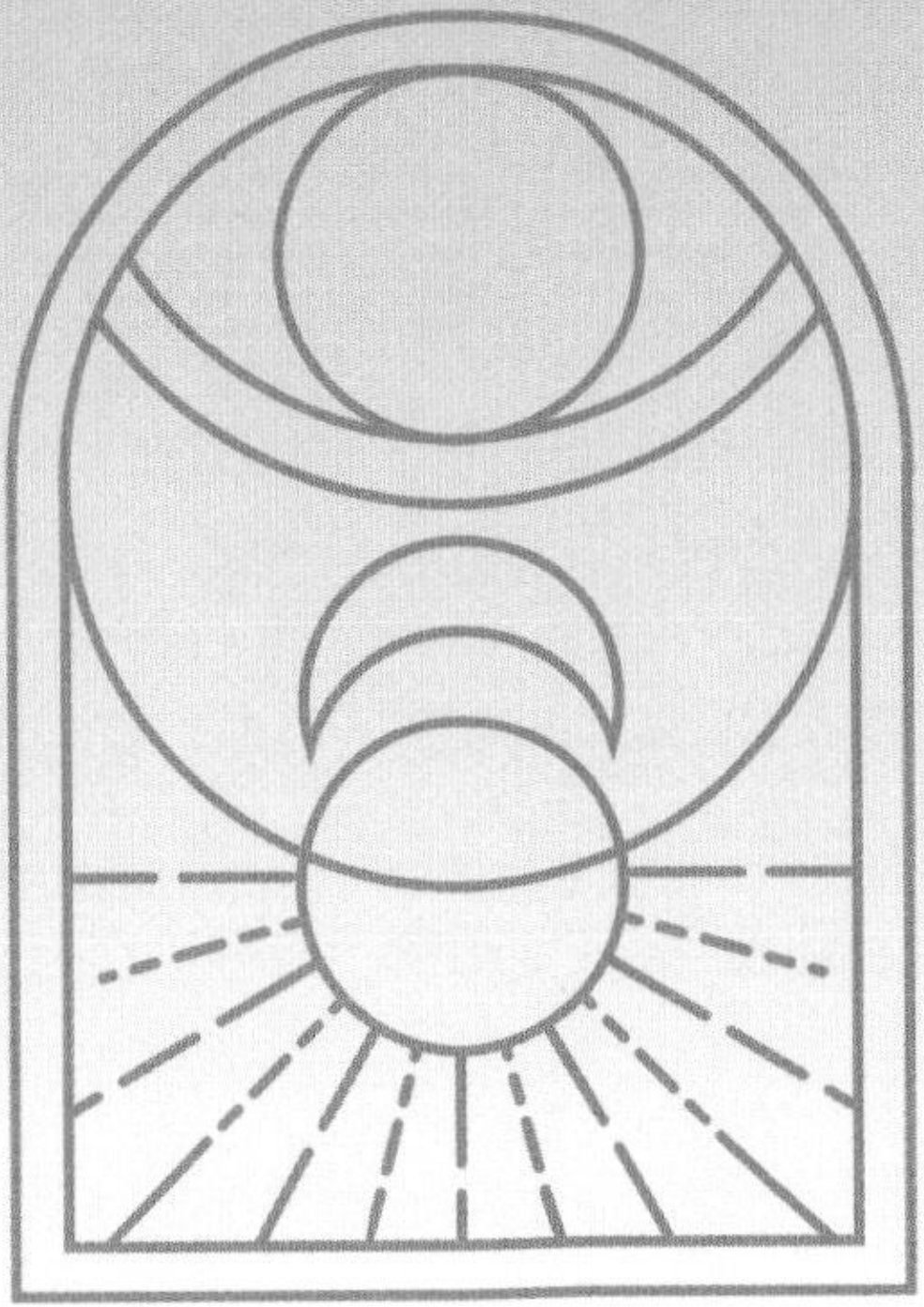

Intimacy requires courage because risk is inescapable.

ROLLO MAY

NO BIRD SOARS TOO HIGH IF HE SOARS WITH HIS OWN WINGS.

WILLIAM BLAKE

CONVERSATION is the most human and HUMANIZING thing we do.

SHERRY TURKLE

MANDALA

P.O. Box 3088
San Rafael, CA 94912
www.MandalaEarth.com

CEO: Raoul Goff
Editorial Director: Katie Killebrew
VP Creative: Chrissy Kwasnik
VP Manufacturing: Alix Nicholaeff
Associate Art Director: Ashley Quackenbush
Designer: Amy DeGrote
Project Editor: Claire Yee
Production Manager: Andy Harper

© 2022 Mandala Publishing. All rights reserved. No part of this book may be reproduced in any form without written permission from the publisher.

978-1-64722-579-7
Manufactured in China by Insight Editions
10 9 8 7 6 5 4 3 2 1
2022 2023 2024